How To Make The Most Of Being Single

51 GOOD THINGS TO DO WHILE YOU'RE WAITING FOR THE RIGHT ONE TO COME ALONG

HAROLD IVAN SMITH

How To Make The Most Of Being Single

51 GOOD THINGS TO DO WHILE YOU'RE WAITING FOR THE RIGHT ONE TO COME ALONG

BROADMAN
&HOLMAN
PUBLISHERS

Nashville, Tennessee

© Copyright 1994
Broadman & Holman Publishers
All rights reserved

4253-65
0-8054-5365-2

Dewey Decimal Classification: 305.9
Subject Heading: SINGLE PEOPLE
Library of Congress Card Catalog Number: 94-498
Printed in the United States of America

Unless otherwise noted, Scripture quotations are from the Holy Bible, *New International Version*, copyright © 1973, 1978, 1984 by International Bible Society. Scripture quotations marked (KJV) are from the *King James Version* of the Bible, and (CEV) from the *Contemporary English Version*, copyright © American Bible Society 1991, 1992, used by permission.

Library of Congress Cataloging-in-Publication Data

Smith, Harold Ivan, 1947 —
    51 good things to do while you're waiting for the right one to come along / by Harold Ivan Smith
        p. cm.
    ISBN 0-8054-5365-2
    1. Single people—United States—Miscellanea.   I. Title.   II. Title: Fifty-one good things to do while you're waiting for the right one to come along.
HQ800.4U6S634   1994
305.9'0652—dc20   94-498
                                                                                                    CIP

Dedication

To Sandy West
Junction City, Kansas,
whose incredible commitment
as a lay volunteer
in single adult ministry
in a small town is remarkable.

To Betty Benjestorf
Fallbrook, California,
whose incredible commitment
as a lay volunteer
in single adult ministry
was remarkable.

Sandy and Betty have modeled
compassion, vision, and care—
often going
the second, third, and
fourth miles.

Sandy's and Betty's work with
adults who are single
illustrates the word servant.

Contents

Introduction. 1
1. Volunteer. 6
2. Learn to Be a Cheerful Giver 8
3. Clip Newspaper/Magazine Articles. 10
4. Host Manly Evenings and Ladies' Pizza Nites. 12
5. Get a Dog. 14
6. Give up the Late News on TV or Radio 16
7. Sing at Home or in Your Car 18
8. Join a Community Service Organization 20
9. Read to a Child 22
10. Listen More, Interrupt Less 24
11. Celebrate Your Doxology Day 26
12. Write a Letter to the Editor 28
13. Read Obituaries 30
14. Teach Someone to Read 32
15. Give Money to Someone's Dream 34

Contents

16. Smile at Children/Listen to Children 36
17. Befuddle Someone 38
18. Plant a Tree, a Shrub, or a Bush in Someone's Memory 40
19. Really Look 42
20. Really Taste 44
21. Really Touch 46
22. Really Smell 48
23. Really Feel 50
24. Sink Your Roots Deep into a Community 52
25. Ask Before Buying: Do I Really Need This? 54
26. Treat a Senior Single Adult to a Meal 56
27. Celebrate a "Lite" Christmas 58
28. Give Away "Stuff" to Good Causes 60
29. Read Historical Markers 62
30. Make the Most of Sundays 64
31. Go Back to School 66
32. Enjoy, Explore, Protect Nature .68
33. Respect Your Body 70
34. Laugh . . . Tell Jokes 72
35. Visit Cemeteries 74
36. Forgive! 76

37. Say "I'm Sorry" 78
38. Park Farther out in Parking Lots 80
39. Treasure Your Uniqueness 82
40. Be a Secret Robin Hood 84
41. Travel 86
42. Send Lots of Greeting Cards 88
43. Teach a Bible Study Class 90
44. Get out of Debt 92
45. Get to Know Single Adults in the Bible 94
46. Write Your Will 96
47. Tip Well and Smile at Servers 98
48. Bake 100
49. Live as Though What You Do Makes a Difference 102
50. Remember Your Priorities 104
51. Set Goals 106
Some Final Words 108
Answers 111
Notes 112

Introduction

How many times have you heard the question, "Why isn't a nice person like you married?" How do you answer?

"Beats me. I wish I knew."

"Ahhhhhhh . . ." Or "Wellllll . . ."

"No one deserves as much love as I could give!"

If the questioner stops at that point, you're ahead, but generally he has a follow-up question or offers the name of a person "you should meet" or "shares" a Scripture promise about God's timing.

Some want to know when you are going to "settle down and get married." If some of us get any more settled down, we may never marry. We would have to unsettle to say, "I do."

There are many reasons people do not marry; some are simple: "No one ever asked me." Others are more emotionally and psychologically complex or troublesome. For some people, it's an unexplainable mystery. Many single adults are not willing to lower their standards to get married. One of my friends asks, "I know what you're looking for, but what will you settle for?"

Every day single adults get tired of waiting and ask the question, "Is this the best I can do?" Too often the answer is, "You'll do" rather than "I do."

So a lot of single adults are "on hold," waiting like the little blinking light on the answering machine, waiting for the tardy Prince or Princess Charming to come riding into their life and whisk them away to the magical land called "marriage."

Waiting for the right one to show up... a feeling Nancy Honeytree captured in her song, "Still Single After All These Years!" Some of us are not good at waiting. We're impatient. Any encounter with the opposite sex causes us to wonder if this could be the one. Generally, when traveling, I carry a couple of books or a file of correspondence in case my plane is delayed. It's what Scripture describes as "redeeming the time." Of course, waiting for the right one to come along is a little more complicated than waiting for a plane. But are you redeeming the time? the season?

As a single adult, do you wait well?

Comic Robin Williams captured the attention of many singles by his portrayal of a poet/teacher in *The Dead Poet's Society* with the phrase, *carpe diem*, meaning seize the day. I think single adults should *carpe tempus*! Seize the season.

That's what *51 Things* is about—waiting actively rather than passively. Too many single adults regularly host pity parties and moan, sometimes melodramatically but always loudly enough for the world to hear, "Poor me! If only someone had married me and made me a whole person!"

In one of my early books I wrote, "Even if I never meet you, I am going to be happy with the me I will live with until I meet you, unless I meet you first." You may need to read that a couple of times. I ... will ... be ... happy ...

with ... the ... me ... I ... will ... live ... with! I have to learn to be happy with my me and with this season called singleness. Otherwise, I will make a nuisance of myself and further contribute to the negative stereotypes so many people have about singleness.

Single adults make a big mistake in waiting to be rescued from their singleness. In *The On-Purpose Person*, Kevin McCarthy said there are three types of adults in the river called life: *Floaters, fighters,* and *navigators.* "(*Floaters* passively resign themselves to accept the river [singleness] in its present condition... They aimlessly go along for the ride whichever direction the river takes."[1]

On Sunday mornings near the coffee and donuts you will hear litanies of dateless weekends of how unfair the opposite sex is to miss out on a chance for a date. "*Fighters* fight the realities of singleness. They flail against the river, trying to control it."[2]

On Sundays they are nearly exhausted from everything they have done that week to keep from confronting any reminder of their singleness. They stay busy and try to keep their minds off their naked ring fingers.

Navigators recognize they cannot control the river. The best they can do is equip themselves for the adventure of singleness. They accept the reality of singleness and find ways to make the most of this season's opportunities.[3]

You may not want to be single or single-again, but if you are reading this book, you are probably single. Are you open to some flexible advice? When I attended a calligraphy exhibit in Salem, Oregon, I broke into laughter as I read:

> Be What
>
> You Is—
>
> Cuz If
>
> You Be
>
> What You
>
> Ain't
>
> Then You
>
> Ain't What
>
> You Is!

This epitaph was found on the gravestone of a frontier gunslinger who was a wee bit slow in his last gunfight.

Singleness is not a prison sentence to be served with time off for good behavior.

Singleness is an adventure. Single adults have two trustable "scouts." Jesus and the apostle Paul were both single. We also have a long succession of people through the centuries who came to terms with their singleness. They probably wanted to be married as much as you do, and they probably asked their share of questions, yet they chose to live in the reality of their singleness and made the world a better place. It's a Who's Who . . .

> Lottie Moon
>
> George Frederick Handel
>
> Annie Armstrong
>
> Wilbur and Orville Wright
>
> Susan B. Anthony
>
> Admiral John Paul Jones
>
> Jane Addams
>
> Robert E. B. Baylor
>
> Dorothea Dix
>
> David Brainerd

Christina Rossetti

Raoul Wallenberg

Elizabeth Blackwell

James Buchanan

Charlotte Elliott

Mother Clara Hale

Alfred Nobel

Sometimes we spend so much time looking for the right person to marry that we fail to become the person we should be.

This book offers practical suggestions for not wasting the precious season called singleness. Each chapter offers one suggestion. Following the suggestion is a trivia question about single adults who have changed their world. Test your knowledge ... the answers may surprise you. Each chapter also includes a quotation from a well known single.

Why 51 things? you ask. Why not 52; one for every week of the year? If you need 52, here's the last thing to do— take a week off. Recharge. Restore yourself.

1 Volunteer

"Don't just sit there like a bump on a log. Do something!" That's what my father told me on more than one occasion when I said that I was bored. Get involved. Volunteer.

Alice Eastwood did during the great San Francisco quake of 1906, as the flames got closer to the California Academy of Sciences, she realized the Institute's collection of rare botanical samples was endangered, but what could one woman do? This botanist rushed in, quickly recruited six volunteers, raced up six floors of crumbling steps, and saved the collection. Meanwhile, Alice's own house burned to the ground.[1]

A recent Gallup Poll showed "that many Americans are willing to volunteer but are not being asked."[2] So, go ahead and volunteer. And if you are asked to volunteer, say, "Yes."

This single adult Sunday School teacher's life was turned around when someone said, "Why don't you do something about tuberculosis?" during the nationwide TB epidemic in 1907. "Me? I do my thing every Sunday morning from 9:30 to 10:30. Besides, I'm not a doctor or nurse or scientist!" When she encouraged the U.S. postmaster general to sell stamps to raise money, he instead gave her permission to recruit volunteers to sell nongovernment-issued stamps in the Wilmington, Delaware, post office. _____ designed the first American Christmas seal: A holly garland around the Red Cross with the words, "Merry Christmas." Friends paid for fifty thousand of the stamps to be printed. On December 7, 1907, this single adult began selling Christmas seals for a penny each. That first year she and her volunteers raised $3,000; in 1908, they raised $135,000. The American Lung Association raises $40 million each year through Christmas seals. Who was this single adult?[3]

"Never turn down a job because you think it's too small, you don't know where it can lead."
—Julia Morgan[4]

2

Learn to Be a Cheerful Giver

It happened in the parking lot of Lamar's Donuts, where they make the best donuts in the world. I was minding my own business, enjoying my peanut butter long johns and the *Kansas City Star*. A gentleman walked up to my car and said, "Please, mister, my mother and I don't have anything to eat, and I was wondering if you could . . ." I had already decided I could give him some pocket change when he said, "spare ten dollars."

I couldn't believe his nerve, but he immediately dropped his request before I could even sputter. "Five dollars. We need groceries. I'll pay you back. I live down the street."

What was I to do? If I had eaten my donuts while I was driving, this wouldn't have happened. I felt the man was bothering me.

I gave him the five dollars, finished my donuts, and drove to the airport, mumbling. *Imagine asking a total stranger for ten dollars! Why did I give him the money? My "token" good deed for the week? How could I have said no while eating donuts? What if everything he had told me was true? What if he was hungry? I could have shared a donut, but he might not have liked peanut butter donuts.*

The real struggle erupted hours later when I realized I had not given the five dollars with a smile. I had stingily, reluctantly given, I remember my first grade Sunday School teacher saying, "The Lord loves a cheerful giver."

What would Jesus have done at Lamar's? I'm not certain. I know something He once said, "Whatever you did for one of the least of these . . . you did for Me" (Matt. 25:40). Today there are a lot of "least of these" on the street. Am I not diminished if I ignore them? Maybe they will use the money I give them unwisely, but that's their issue. My task is to give as generously and "cheerfully" as I can.

In 1887, Queen Victoria had ruled the British Empire for fifty years. A single adult merchant wrote, "I take the liberty of writing to inquire whether your most gracious Majesty would accept the largest cheese ever made" (11,200 pounds). An aide replied, "The Queen could not accept presents from private individuals to whom she was not personally known."

_____ passed the letters to the newspapers and won a public relations coup; within two years he would be a millionaire and a household name in England. Who was this single adult merchant?[1]

> "I have learned in my years on earth to hold everything loosely, because when I hold them tightly, God has to pry my fingers away, and that hurts."
> —Corrie ten Boom[2]

3

Clip Newspaper/ Magazine Articles

You've finished with your newspaper or new magazine. How do you know there isn't something in there that would be valuable to your pastor, single adult minister, or to a friend? Try clipping items and mailing them with a with a note attached, saying, "Did you see this?" or "I thought you might find this interesting."

Recently, my friend, Phyllis, sent me an article about four Houston bachelors who advertised for wives using a billboard. After all, 192,000 vehicles passed the billboard every day. Who knows? I would not have seen the article otherwise, since it wasn't big news in Kansas City.

Sometimes while reading we get distracted and have to ask, "Now where was I?" and may overlook a news item or personal interest story that would have been valuable for future use. It's wonderful when a friend clips it and sends it to us.

Much of American economic theory ties back to this British economist and single adult. As a young adult, _____ taught logic and moral development and was a specialist on the concept of sympathy. He argued in the 1750s that "each person must scrutinize his own feelings and behaviors with the same strictness that he employs when considering those of others." Yet, he is remembered for his conviction that the "wealth of a nation is to be gauged by the number and variety of consumable goods." His book, *The Wealth of Nations*, made the term "laissez-faire" a well-admired concept among politicians. Who was this single adult?[1]

"I realize now there would not have been any way I could have:

> *Read the books I have read*
> *Written the words I have written*
> *Gone to the places I have gone*
> *Studied the courses I have studied*
> *Learned the languages I have learned*
> *Maintained the schedule I have maintained*
> *Mended the people I have mended*

if I had been encumbered by a husband and family. Perhaps my life's greatest tribute was paid to me by my mother when she declared, "You have done what I wish I could have done!"
> —*Evelyn Ramsey*[2]

4

Host Manly Evenings and Ladies' Pizza Nites

My friend, Dave Sanders, began sponsoring "manly" evenings about eight years ago. He invited men, both single and married, to come to his home for a couple of hours of food, videos, and socializing. For some non-Christians, this was a great way to be around Christians. Dave keeps the food simple—pizza, salad, dessert—and everyone brings something. Dave calls this "giving them part of the evening," and it motivates everyone to show up.

The evenings became so popular that female friends began asking, "What about us?" So, Dave started "Ladies' Pizza Nights" but discovered females preferred to talk rather than watch videos.

Several times a year invitations go out, and forty people show up for a wonderful evening in Dave's home. These nights have made David's singleness much richer. Why not try this yourself?

This single adult came to New Orleans about 1768. As a peddler, he traveled over the Mississippi Valley. He eventually bought a plantation in Point Coupee Parish and developed trading posts that made him quite prosperous. He had intended to return to his native France, but after the French Revolution, he decided to stay in Louisiana.

_____ became widely known for his philanthropy, piety, and morality. He loved to entertain. After the Louisiana Purchase, he became involved in public service, serving as president of the Constitutional Convention in 1812 and later in the Louisiana senate.

His will left plans to free all the slaves on his six plantations and to provide retirement for those over the age of sixty. He left a great deal of money to charities, but his most stunning provision was the money he left to provide dowries for poor girls in West Baton Rouge and Point Coupee parishes; otherwise, many could never have married. One hundred years after his death young women still benefitted from his generosity. Who was this single adult?[1]

> "Being an old maid is like death by drowning, a really delightful sensation after you cease to struggle."
> —Edna Ferber[2]

5 Get a Dog

Dogs have been described as man's best friend, and many singles have found this to be true. Many ex-singles report they met the right one while walking their dog. People are fascinated by big or unusual dogs and often ask, "What kind of dog is that?" or "What's your dog's name?" or "Does he bite?"

Dogs can be great to come home to, especially if they have been well trained and if you have chosen a dog that fits your personality. They may also offer you or your mother, who worries about you, a sense of security. One of my single friends always leaves the stereo tuned to a classical station when he's gone, claiming his dog enjoys the music while he is gone.

For those of you who are cat lovers, cats offer the same benefits dogs do. They are also quieter and more self-sufficient.

This scientist broke all the stereotypes. As a professor at the University of Washington, she was an early environmentalist, directing a study of the damage done to dry docks, ships, and wharves by marine animals. She was an early protester against the destructive impact upon oceans caused by the dumping of domestic and industrial wastes, pesticides, and radioisotopes. She took six buildings left over from the 1962 Seattle World's Fair and turned them into the Pacific Science Center with the goal of making science "inviting to those who may view it as a forbidding domain of the intellectually elite."

In 1972 she was appointed by President Nixon to be a member of the Atomic Energy Commission. She said, "I was appointed because I was a woman" but quickly demonstrated she did not intend to be a token member. A year later, _____ became head of the AEC with a budget of $3 billion, charged with supervising the development of nuclear weapons as well as the civilian use of nuclear power. The position brought her into conflict with another single adult, Ralph Nader, who labeled her "Ms. Plutonium." During her tenure at AEC, she lived in a motor home designed to accommodate her books and her two dogs, Ghille, a one-hundred-pound Scottish deerhound, and Jacques, a miniature poodle, her constant companions even in her AEC office. In 1976 she was elected governor of Washington State. Who was this single adult scientist/activist?[1]

> "The frontiers are not east or west, north or south, but wherever a man fronts a fact."
>
> —Henry David Thoreau[2]

6

Give up the Late News on TV or Radio

Americans are addicted to the news. Some singles watch the late news and often go to bed with the radio on in case botulism breaks out in Bostwana during the night. First thing in the morning we turn on a news show to start our days. Our local paper and *USA Today* bring us up to date on anything we might have missed.

The psalmist, who didn't have to deal with late news, wrote, "I will lie down and sleep in peace, for You alone, O Lord, make me dwell in safety" (Ps. 4:8). We might be able to serve the Lord better if we didn't have all those little snippets of news: Murders, assaults, vehicular homicides, drive-by shootings, tax increases, layoffs, and miscellaneous mayhem bouncing around in our minds, making us worry about things over which we have no control. If it is important, we'll hear about it the next morning.

Four men have lived a portion of their days in the White House as single adults: Jefferson was a widower; Wilson remarried in the White House. Two men were elected as bachelors. Only one remained a bachelor during his four years at 1600 Pennsylvania Avenue. In fact, his political career began after a failed romance. _____ was so despondent following the death of his ex-fiance that friends pushed him to run for Congress in 1821 to distract him from his grief. After ten years in the House and eleven in the Senate and stints as Ambassador to Great Britain and Russia and Secretary of State, he was elected President in 1856. His most important achievement may have been holding the Union together long enough for Lincoln to be elected. Who was this single adult?[1]

> "I think something is dangerous only if you are not prepared for it or if you don't have control over it, or if you can't think how to get yourself out of it."
>
> —Judith Resnik[2]

7

Sing at Home or in Your Car

You're right. I haven't heard you sing! But we're not talking about joining the choir, just singing from the hymnal. Next to their Bibles, Christians have valued their hymnals. No wonder. Jesus' coming was heralded by an angel chorus that filled the heavens with "Glory to God in the highest, and on earth peace, good will toward men."

You may say you're unfamiliar with the words. If you have a hymnal at home, you can become familiar with them. Humorist Lewis Grizzard recalled attending a Christmas Eve service. "We were asked to sing the first and third verses of some ponderous hymn with which I was not familiar. And across from it in the hymnbook was 'Away in the Manger.' I know all the words to 'Away in the Manger,' but we didn't sing that. . . . I want to sing, 'Precious Memories,' and 'When the Roll Is Called Up Yonder,' and 'Dwelling in Beulahland' from that old brown hymnal."[1]

You can also pray the hymnal. Take a classic like "Have Thine Own Way, Lord." Instead of singing the verses, pray them, pausing now and then to reflect.

Churches would not have as much to sing if single adults had not been such prolific hymn writers. In fact, there is a tradition called "the spinster hymn writers," never-marrieds who wrote hundreds of hymns and gospel songs. Guess who wrote the following:

_____ "Angels, from the Realms of Glory"

_____ "Take My Life and Let It Be"

_____ "When I Survey the Wondrous Cross"

_____ "O Love That Will Not Let Me Go"

_____ "I Love to Tell the Story"

_____ "Joy to the World"

_____ "There Is a Fountain Filled with Blood"

_____ "I Need Thee Every Hour"

_____ "Have Thine Own Way, Lord"

_____ "Now Thank We All Our God"

The list could go on. And somewhere today a single adult is writing a hymn or gospel song or chorus we will soon be singing.

> *"I would rather be an anonymous author of a few hymns which should become an imperishable inheritance to the people of God, than bequeath another epic poem to the world, which would rank my name with Homer, Virgil, or Milton."*
> —James Montgomery[2]

8

Join a Community Service Organization

During the summer of 1993, when severe flooding swamped much of the Midwest, I discovered a whole new meaning to the concept of neighborhood, service, and volunteering. The symbol of the summer was a sandbag, held open by one, filled by another, tied off by a third, and then handed down a long row of volunteers. Each bag counted.

Over the past decades we have been so busy singing "I Did It My Way" that we forgot about community involvement. We forgot how much we really do need each other.

There are community organizations in your area that need your time, energy, and creativity as well as your financial assistance. Get involved in an organization committed to making your community a better, more compassionate place.

This single adult founded one of New Jersey's first "free" public schools and may have been the first regularly appointed woman in the civil service. When the Civil War broke out, she collected supplies for soldiers, often spending her own money. _____ spent most of 1865 looking for missing soldiers and marking graves.

After a nervous breakdown, she went to Europe to recover and discovered the International Committee of the Red Cross.

In 1881 she founded the American Association of the Red Cross and served as president until 1904, offering relief for domestic disasters such as floods, fires, epidemics, and accidents. At age seventy-seven, she rode mule wagons as a nurse in the Spanish-American War. Who was this community-minded single adult?[1]

> "Were there none who were discontented with what they have, the world would never reach anything better."
>
> —Florence Nightingale[2]

9

Read to a Child

If you've attended one of my seminars, you know I start every session with a children's story. Why? Well, because I understand children's stories: they are fun to read, and they disarm audiences. I love *Ira Sleeps Over; Alexander and the Terrible; Horrible, No Good, Very Bad Day; The Velveteen Rabbit; Love You Forever;* and of course, the *Frog and Toad* stories.

I enjoy reading to children even though I do not have children of my own. Taking time to read to a child and to encourage the child to read is a gift. We be-moan declining reading skills, but we have forgotten that a love of reading must be modeled. Say to a child, "Would you like me to read you a story?" or "I'd love to hear you read." Give books to children for birthdays, Christmas, or for no special reason.

Early in life this single adult was described as "a book hungry" girl. In 1887 she enrolled in the recently opened school of library science at Columbia University. In 1890 she began her work at the library of the Pratt Institute in Brooklyn. When the new library was built under her design, an innovation caught the public by surprise: This was the first library in the country with a children's room in the original plan, fully recognizing children as library patrons. In 1911 she became head of the library school at the New York Public Library and helped train thousands of librarians.

_____ also made time to help small libraries, particularly through her book, *Hints to Small Libraries*. Would the new public library in my neighborhood have such a glorious space for children if it had not been for this single adult's innovations? Who was she?[1]

> "In primitive communities, the kraal or tent or cave or camp would contain old and young, adults and children. Everyone needed everyone. Everyone still needs everyone, but in our present segregated activities and segregated residences, singles may not always realize how much they need children and how much children need them."
>
> —*Elva McAllaster*[2]

10 Listen More, Interrupt Less

Have you ever been out on a date and the only station your companion was tuned to was KW*ME*? Have you ever listened to a seemingly endless recitation of facts, achievements, accomplishments, and goals? Or have you ever had to call someone because you've forgotten what they said? "Uh...refresh my memory...." Sometimes we don't listen well.

James McGinnis has some excellent listening guidelines. He suggests, "We might think of fasting from words instead of fasting from food." He suggests singles listen before speaking, be the last rather than the first to speak in a group or committee, ask others for their opinions before offering their own, and resist the temptation to say "no" before they have heard the person out.[1] Another important guideline is to look at the speaker. We hear with our ears, but we listen with our eyes and hearts as well as with our ears.

The best relationships are formed between two people who have the ability to really listen. It's a lost art in our communications-oriented culture. If you are seeking meaningful relationships, you must learn to listen as well as talk.

Women gained the right to vote in federal elections with the ratification of the Nineteenth Amendment to the U.S. Constitution by the Tennessee Legislature (it was the thirty-sixth state to ratify) in August 1920. The Amendment passed by one vote, and that vote was cast by a single adult who had changed his mind after earlier voting against the Amendment. Rumors circulated in Nashville that _____ changed his mind after a "conversation" with a "rat," a term for one of the young single women actively lobbying for the ratification of the Amendment. This courageous young legislator, who would lose his seat in the next election because of this vote, stood in the House to announce that indeed he had "listened" to a woman and had changed his mind because of her influence. The woman was his mother. "I know that a mother's advice is always the safest for her boy to follow, and my mother wanted me to vote for ratification."

Fifty years later, he said, "I am glad that I was able to do something for the millions of fine American women." Who was this single adult?[2]

> *"The first service that one owes to others in the fellowship consists in listening to them. . . . Many people are looking for an ear that will listen. They do not find it among Christians, because these Christians are talking when they should be listening. But he who can no longer listen to his brother will soon no longer be listening to God either."*
>
> —*Dietrich Bonhoeffer*[3]

11 Celebrate Your Doxology Day

You're probably wondering, "Just exactly what is Doxology Day?" Well, my good friend, Elva McAllaster, came up with the idea in 1979. Doxology Day is an occasion to celebrate your singleness. "Oh." I hear you groan, "You've got to be kidding! Celebrate my singleness?!!!" Well, why not? If you were married, you would be celebrating your anniversary, so why not celebrate your singleness? After all, it's downright biblical. Paul, who knew a few things about being single, wrote, "Always giving thanks to God the Father for everything" (Eph. 5:20). "Everything" includes singleness.

When do you celebrate Doxology Day? Six months from your birthday.

How do you spend your Doxology Day? Celebrate. Eat out. Take a long hot bath. Take the day off—just tell your boss, "It's my Doxology Day." Treat yourself to something special, and set aside some time with a piece of paper and pencil to compose a list of the blessings God has bestowed on you: health, a job, friends, a good home, a skill or craft. We have many things to be grateful for.

Mother's Day is the third most celebrated holiday in the world; only Christmas and Easter are more popular. This single adult's mother had often said she hoped someday, someone would start a special day to honor the nation's mothers. After her mother's death in 1905, _____ launched a crusade to organize a national Mother's Day. She traveled, made speeches, wrote letters to persons of influence, and in 1908 organized the first Mother's Day celebration in Grafton, West Virginia (her birthplace), and in Philadelphia. In 1914 President Woodrow Wilson proclaimed the second Sunday in May should be celebrated as Mother's Day.

Why the second Sunday? It was the day closest to this single adult's mother's death. To encourage people to wear carnations, she would stand on a street corner with a big tub of them. As people walked by, she asked them to wear the flower as a tribute to their mothers: Red if the mother was living and white if the mother was deceased. It all began with a single adult and a single idea. Who was this single adult?[1]

> "Well, Lord, if this is the end of my life, I'll just have to say how thankful I am, and what a wonderful privilege it's been, but if it's your will for me to live, then I just give myself to you all the more. To the best of my strength."
> —General Eva Burrows[2]

12 Write a Letter to the Editor

One of the important traditions in this country is the free press and, particularly, the freedom to write to the editor of a magazine or your local newspaper. It's one of the oldest ways to "express yourself." Your letter could influence others and maybe even bring about positive change.

Perhaps there is some burning issue in your community or some issue that needs to be a burning one. If you think your newspaper's coverage on an issue has not been fair or adequate or balanced, that's your cue to write.

Published articles on single adults may be promoting the "swinging single" image or may have presented single adults as self-centered. Thoughtful letters to the editor challenging that viewpoint are important. Your opinion counts. So let us hear you or, better still, read you.

A couple of hints. Be brief. Be clear. Be kind. Too many Christians think a letter to the editor should have as many Scripture verses as possible. If you follow these guidelines, your letter could help make a difference in people's thoughts or actions.

This nation would not celebrate Thanksgiving as a holiday if it had not been for the persistent letter-writing of this single parent. Her husband died in 1822 and left her with five children; after publishing her first novel, *Northwood*, she moved to Boston in 1827 to edit a ladies' magazine and eventually attracted the attention of Louis Godey, who made her the first editor of *Godey's Lady's Book*, the widely read magazine devoted to "female improvement."

Every year she personally wrote to the governors of the states, proposing they declare a Thanksgiving holiday; she used the editorial pages of the magazine to lobby the wives of decision makers to support the issue. Many rejected the idea out of concern for separation of church and state. By 1859 thirty states had Thanksgiving celebrations on the last Thursday of November; however, _____ wanted a national holiday proclaimed by the President and celebrated in all the states.

On October 2, 1863, her persistence in letter-writing paid off. On the heels of the decisive Union victory at Gettysburg, Lincoln wanted to do something to celebrate. Secretary of State Seward, who had been governor of New York for eight years before the war and who had received eight of this single adult's letters, suggested, "Why not have a day of national celebration of Thanksgiving?" Lincoln agreed and proclaimed a national day to give thanks to God. Who was this single parent?[1]

> "Lord, it is enough that You alone see and I know who I am what I am doing. It is enough that You are aware of what my life as a single person is all about."
> —Susan Muto [2]

29

13 Read Obituaries

I read the obits. If I don't find my name included, I know it's going to be a good day. Most singles leave this section for "later." A lot later. Why read obits? Well, they remind you that death is a reality, that none of us know how much time we have. Obits encourage us, in Jonathan Swift's words, "to live all the days of our lives."

I was fascinated by an article in the *Orlando Sentinel* written by Lisa Scott, a homemaker with two young children. She reads the obituaries as a way of answering the question, "Can I really make a difference?"

"Obituaries," says Lisa, "tell me briefly of homemakers, laborers, secretaries, technicians, nurses, teachers. People like me and like you, people who worked hard, loved their families, tried to improve their lots, and sometimes failed." What's the point? "The real movers and shakers are those of us who live quiet lives, are honest with ourselves and others, and who respect our place in the world even as we may try to change it."[1] So, tomorrow morning, give the obits a once-over.

This single adult reminds us our choices create our obituaries and eulogies. _____ was the first woman elected to a statewide office in Kansas; she served as superintendent of public instruction from 1918 to 1922, assuming the office after a long career in teaching and writing textbooks; her texts were as common in the Midwest as the McGuffey Readers were elsewhere. Despite a busy schedule, she managed to graduate from law school and make money investing in real estate.

As head of the public schools, she declared war on drinking, card playing, high hemlines, dancing, and many other misbehaviors that attracted her fury. "Wipe that paint off your face," she bullied one teacher. "Lower that hem!" she ordered another.

Although she proposed many good innovations, her incessant "ranting and raving" about conduct turned her into a public laughingstock. She was defeated for reelection and lost a later race for attorney general of Kansas.

She died in extreme poverty at age eighty-two in 1953 with a rather meager obituary. Who was this single adult?[2]

"Live so as to be missed."
—Robert Murray McCheyne[3]

14 Teach Someone to Read

I was stunned by the newspaper headline, "Half of Adults Lack Basic Literacy Skills." Sadly, many adults cannot read a letter explaining a credit card error, figure out a bus schedule, calculate the difference between full price and sale price, or read a complicated menu.

Dr. Frank C. Laubach, founder of the Laubach Literacy Program, observed, "They are the silent victims, the forgotten people."[1] Somewhere near you is a Laubach Literacy Council (see the Yellow Pages or contact the local school board)

that will train you as a volunteer so you can teach someone to read. There are no specific educational requirements, no experience needed. You just need the ability to read, patience, and a few hours each week to tutor. As you read this, potential readers are waiting for someone to volunteer. What a gift you could offer them!

This Southern woman was expected to marry well; however, a Sunday afternoon experience in her playhouse on her father's Georgia plantation changed her life course. Three mountain children showed up outside, and she invited them in, entertaining them by telling Bible stories. Each Sunday they returned with friends until there were forty. Before long _____ had to move to a dilapidated church in Possum Trot. By age thirty she decided to devote her life to teaching mountain children in northern Georgia "a way to help themselves." In 1902 she opened a school for boys and helped the state found eleven similar schools. This single adult relied on the generosity of individuals like Henry Ford (who eventually gave $4 million), Andrew Carnegie, and Theodore Roosevelt to supplement her personal giving.

Then she decided the boys she educated needed "suitable" wives who had also received an education. Against her board's advice, she opened a school for girls in 1909. In 1926 those schools were organized as a junior college and in 1930 as a senior college. The "_____" way of self-help, plain living, and close ties to the north Georgia culture changed the economic composition of the region.

Thousands of Georgians got a chance in life because of this single adult. Readers of *Good Housekeeping* voted her one of the twelve greatest living Americans. The motto on her desk read, "Prayer changes things." Who was this single adult who was often a bridesmaid in her graduates' weddings?[2]

> "I have learned to live each day as it comes, and not to borrow trouble by dreading tomorrow. It is the dark menace of the future that makes cowards of us."
>
> —Dorothea Dix[3]

15

Give Money to Someone's Dream

I buy candy from every kid that knocks on my door. Maybe it's just payback for all my candy and magazines selling days. Really, selling candy is a way for children to say, "Could you please help me?"

A talented artist did not have money to take art lessons. He could have given up, but he went to a couple of people and said, "Would you be my patron or sponsor?" Those who said yes helped underwrite the cost of his art lessons (less than one hundred dollars). Many people today have the paintings of this promising artist student on their walls. Perhaps you might join with others, get behind a dream, and lift it off the ground.

This single adult was born into a wealthy family, traveled in Europe, owned fine art and antiquities, but lived with her sister as a recluse. At seventy-three she became interested in astronomy. In 1888, she read an article by noted American astronomer, Simon Newcomb, who declared almost all major astronomical discoveries of significance had already been made. "We'll see about that!" _____ said, reaching for her checkbook. Her first check, for $50,000, went to Harvard to establish a photographic telescope.

She also dispatched a note to Dr. Newcomb, dismissing his limited perspective, "I think we are only beginning!" Throughout the remainder of her life, this single adult's checkbook supported many astronomers at critical stages in their research. Without her understanding of their dreams, this nation might never have sent a man to the moon. Who was this single adult?

> "Throughout my career, I've been trying to show that science is not just for the scientist. Science is like music. It's too wonderful a world to leave to the specialists."
> —Dixie Ray[2]

35

16 Smile at Children/ Listen to Children

Have you heard that some children in Washington, D.C., are planning their funerals? They are so overwhelmed by the violence of the world that they're losing hope. Single adults have a chance to become actively and creatively involved with children.

Admittedly, this is painful for many singles who want children "of their own." The older you are, the more likely you are to marry someone who has been married and may have children. Some of us hear the steady increasing ticking of the biological clock and know time is running out.

If Jesus, as a single adult, made time for children in His life, how much more do we need to follow His example? How much effort does it take to smile at children, talk to them, or praise them? Let a child interrupt your life. Your life may be enriched by the experience.

This single adult's research ensured many of us lived past childbirth. She was one of the first women graduates of Columbia University Medical School and entered a surgery internship, at the time a field few women entered. After two years, she switched to anesthesiology, convinced a woman could not support herself as a surgeon. She saw anesthesiology as a place where a woman could do pioneer work.

_____ soon headed the department, the first woman to head a specialty at Columbia-Presbyterian Medical Center in New York; in 1949 she became the first woman full professor at Columbia.

However, she gave up her administrative post to focus on research on the effects of anesthesia in childbirth, developing the _____ Scale which evaluated babies' need for special medical care at birth.

She went back to school at age forty-nine to earn a master's degree in public health at Johns Hopkins, then accepted a position as the executive director of the National Foundation for March of Dimes. She spent the rest of her life raising public consciousness for funding research on birth defects. She raised the annual income of the March of Dimes from $19 million in 1959 to more than $46 million at the time of her death.[1]

> "People brought babies to Jesus, hoping He might touch them. When the disciples saw it, they shooed them off. Jesus called them back. 'Let these children alone. Don't get between them and Me. These children are the Kingdom's pride and joy. Mark this: Unless you accept God's Kingdom in the simplicity of a child, you'll never get in.'"
>
> —Jesus (Luke 18:15-17)[2]

17 Befuddle Someone

A lot of boringly predictable people are on the loose in singleland. They are the perpetual complainers and sufferers who are always looking for someone to listen to their problems. Their theme song is "Nobody Knows the Trouble I've Seen."

Too many single adults settle down into predictable ruts and routines: church, work, a night at a restaurant, time at the gym. Well, maybe it's time to lighten up a little.

For my forty-sixth birthday I received a card I treasure. It shows a yard sprinkler going full blast and an adult (certainly old enough to know better) dancing through it. His body English says it all. Why not follow his example. Befuddle. Do something unpredictable or different. Cause a few people to scratch their heads. Don't be so predictable.

This single adult chose to befuddle the British army during the Revolution. When his father died in 1750, he took on the responsibilities of running a large South Carolina plantation; he fought in the militia during the French and Indian War and the Indian skirmishes afterwards. He represented his county in South Carolina's first Provincial Congress; he was one of the first in that colony to take seriously the call for independence from England, and he trained farmers into soldiers. When the Revolution began at Lexington and Concord, _____ was named a captain in the militia; he received an early letter of commendation from General Washington for his daring exploits during a battle near Charleston. During August 1780, this single adult and his guerrillas harassed British positions, at one point winning the release of 150 American prisoners. One angry British general, weary of trying to pin down the captain's ragtags in the swamps, snarled: "Come on, boys. Let's go back. We'll get the Gamecock, but as for this Swamp Fox, the devil himself could not catch him!" The nickname "Swamp Fox" stuck. This single adult and his ragged gang helped defeat the British in the South. Who was he?[1]

> "I never intended to be a celebrity, just an officer in the Navy. I realize I'm awfully lucky the Navy ordered me to that first computer; otherwise, I'd still be a college teacher. It's much more fun being a commodore in the Navy. I just remember my commission says I'm an officer and a gentleman. So, I endeavor to behave like a gentleman."
>
> —Admiral Grace Hooper[2]

18 Plant a Tree, a Shrub, or a Bush in Someone's Memory

Christmas gifts. It is a way to give a family gift.

When I graduated from Peabody College, I was given an iris bulb and told to plant it as a way of remembering my alma mater. Every spring that iris blooms, but I have another Peabody iris in my yard in memory of my good friend, John Moore, who also graduated from Peabody. The iris is a reminder of his influence as a teacher on my life. Planting a tree, shrub, or bush is also a good way to honor the earth. One of my friends gives live plants and trees for birthdays, graduations, and

This single adult grew up in the Salvation Army. By age fifteen (1880) she was a sergeant, and she made captain two years later. Eventually, she headed all The Salvation Army work in London. After a nine-year stint in Canada, she was appointed to supervise all Salvation Army operations in the United States and enhanced its reputation as a major source of social service.

When she wanted to marry another Salvationist, her father objected. When the man she loved challenged him, he retorted, "No more discussion. I have other plans for her." In 1934 this single adult was elected General and headed the worldwide Salvation Army for five years. She often worked and relaxed in her gardens, which were her getaway retreats. Throughout the years, people had given her many plants and trees. named the trees for friends and relatives; she loved to give tours of the grounds, astonishing visitors with her extensive knowledge of information about each tree and plant. Who was this single adult?[1]

WHY I NEVER MARRIED . . .

"First, the man I would marry would have to be handsome. I couldn't live with an ugly man, or an ignorant man. How would he talk to me about the way I live unless he was smart? And he wouldn't marry me to take care of him. He'd have to have heaps of money. . . . Guess he'd have to be deaf, dumb and blind to get married to me."

—*Eartha Mary Magdelene White, at age 95*[2]

---

19 Really Look

How ironic that the opening words of our national anthem are, "O say, can you see...."

I watched small children today at the city market. They walked around pointing with their fingers, excitedly announcing, "Look at . . ." But somewhere en route to adulthood we stop pointing and staring and, in too many cases, looking.

It's so easy to get caught up in our busy lives that we fail to notice what is going on around us. Have you ever admitted in embarrassment, "You know, I hadn't noticed?"

Really look. Three thousand years ago Isaiah talked about people who were always seeing "but never perceiving" (6:9). Sadly, today that's true of a lot of single adults.

To many she was an unruly, undisciplined blind child; but to a remarkable single adult she was an opportunity. Once the word of speech and sight was unlocked through sign language, this young child set out to "look" at the world and to help the disadvantaged. After graduation from Radcliffe, she wrote her autobiography, *The Story of My Life*, which became an overnight best-seller, crusaded for the prevention of ophthalmia neonatorum—the blindness of newborns. First she had to confront the taboo on discussion of the topic, since the affliction was caused by venereal disease. She raised funds for the American Federation for the Blind and successfully lobbied the federal government for legislation on behalf of the blind. She traveled the world and counted its leaders as her friends.

The play, *The Miracle Worker*, chronicled her life and involvement with her teacher, Anne Sullivan Macy. A heroine to the nation's schoolchildren, who was this single adult?[1]

> "Let me read with open eyes the book my days are writing—and learn."
>
> —Dag Hammarskjold[2]

20 Really Taste

In an era of fast food and indigestion, who has time to really taste? It takes too much time to savor food. On many Saturdays when I am home, I like to go to the Farmer's Market and look at all the fresh fruits and vegetables and fresh baked goods. We have been blessed to live in a country with such availability of good food.

Sometimes we overcook and lose the texture of vegetables, or we overseason and lose their natural flavors. I often eat alone finding myself reading a book, shoveling the food into my mouth, seldom taking time to really taste what I have ordered.

Why did God go to so much trouble to make so many vegetables and fruits with such different colors, textures, and tastes? Because He wanted us to enjoy them and to praise Him for His creation.

The next time you are tempted to wolf down a meal, take time for a prayer of thanksgiving for the food, asking God to help you really taste it. It will do wonders for your digestion, and you will eat less, since your taste buds will be satisfied.

Without this single adult, trips to the grocery would be pretty boring. Although she completed the requirements for a degree in chemistry and biology at the University of Pennsylvania, she was denied her degree in 1892 because she was a female. However, they allowed her to take a full class load in the graduate school. Eventually, because she found a technicality in the catalog, she was awarded the Ph.D. in 1895.

_____ was appointed head of Philadelphia's municipal bacteriology labs and wrestled with the problem of the impure milk being sold in the city. After thorough research, she developed standards for milk inspection that were eventually adopted across the country.

She was hired by the Bureau of Chemistry in the USDA only after taking civil service exams under initials rather than her first name. By 1908 she was chief of the food research labs, concentrating on the refrigeration of foods.

In 1922 she resigned her federal job and opened a consulting firm, specializing in frozen foods. She convinced the food industry that through proper freezing methods, fruit, vegetables, and meat could be available year round rather than just in particular growing seasons. There would be no frozen food section, in your grocery stores without this single adult's research and advocacy. Who was she?[1]

> *"The most interesting and important thing in the world is for you to work out your own particular life. . . . Hold your place. Do not try to shift into the place that another occupies. Keep your eye on what you have to work with, not on what somebody else has."*
>
> —Ida Tarbell[2]

21 Really Touch

Touch. The Creator apparently thought touch was important because He lined the surface of our bodies with millions of touch receptacles. Research has demonstrated babies can die if they are not touched. Adults die emotionally without appropriate touch, and the key word here is *appropriate*. In many single adult meetings there is a time for hugs, and some insist on their full quota. Others wander away saying, "Don't Touch Me!"

Use your fingers to feel and capture the fuzz of a fresh peach, the roughness of tree bark, the silk softness of wet roses, the many different textures God has created to invite our loving touch.

Just before my friend Martin died he had lost forty pounds and was skin and bones. He remarked no one ever touched him. When I saw him I wanted to hug him, but I said, "Martin, I am afraid I will hurt you." "Just put your arms around me lightly," he told me.

Sometimes we all need to be touched "lightly."

Have you ever said, "Oh, my aching feet!"? You would be saying it more frequently if it had not been for a single adult who devoted his entire life to feet. As a young shoe salesman in Chicago, he quickly learned many people had foot problems because of the shoes they wore. At age twenty-two, he patented and marketed his first arch support. After selling all day he attended medical school at night, graduating in 1904. Eight years later he founded the Illinois College of Chiropody and Orthopedics, which later became the Illinois College of Podiatric Medicine.

Eventually, _____'s foot products sales jumped from a mere $815 in 1904 to more than a quarter of a billion by 1976. He remained untouched by his success, living in a bachelor's room at the Y.M.C.A. and heading his company until a month before he died at eighty-five. He claimed "never to have forgotten a foot." Who was this single adult?[1]

> "There have been times when I have shared moments of defeat and moments of victory with only a box of Kleenex and the Lord present. It would have been nice to share something with that oue 'special' person; but that person has never existed, so I've formed deep, loving relationships with people around the world. On some of those occasions, when others were occupied with themselves and I felt alone, the Lord has wrapped His arms around me and drawn me into His presence."
>
> —Evelyn Ramsey[2]

22

Really Smell

When I first became single, my widow friend, Eunice Beane, gave me wise words I have tried to follow: have lots of light, lots of color, and lots of good smells. God gifted us with our senses. He wants us to use all of them, not just in restaurants when we say, "What smells sooo good?" (That's one of the problems with fast food. It all smells the same.)

Why did God go to so much trouble to create so many wonderful smells and fragrances? Honeysuckle and fresh roses, Christmas trees? Artificial trees and silk flowers May "look almost real," but they don't smell like the real thing.

Aren't we suckers for new colognes, perfumes, or after shaves? Study the ads. Why, men who use Product X are irresistible. With male logic, some guys thing, "'If a little dab'll do you,' then a whole lot will be perfect." Has your date ever said, "I find you ... overpowering"?

Next time you are tempted to rush to the mall and buy Product X, ask yourself, "What is X going to do that Y and Z didn't?"

Do yourself a favor: Next time you stop to admire the roses, don't just look or touch them, smell them. You may need the memory some wintry day.

This single adult probably had a permanent smell about him of leather and horse because he lived on a horse. But had it not been for the devotion of this man, there might never have been an American Methodist Church. He came to America in 1771, sent as a volunteer missionary by John Wesley. For the next forty-four years, _____ rode between four thousand to six thousand miles a year on horseback. No trail was too rugged, no community too isolated, no village too sin-soaked, that this single or one of his unmarried circuit riders. Who would not consider it a challenge?

In 1784, he was elected the first Bishop of the [then] Methodist Episcopal Church in America. He recruited thousands of unmarried circuit riders because he wanted them available to ride off, at a moment's notice, to the newest section of the American frontier; besides, it was cheaper for the churches. Indeed, the small salaries kept many men from marrying.

By the time of his death in 1816, he was not just the Bishop but also the father of American Methodism. Ten thousand people attended his funeral. Who was this single adult.[1]

> "The horror of that moment," the King went on, "I shall never, never forget!" "You will, though," the Queen said, "if you don't make a memorandum of it."
>
> —Lewis Carroll[2]

23 Really Feel

Have you ever felt like an emotional wreck? Be thankful for that; at least you can feel. These days, many single adults are trying to hide or drown their feelings rather than get in genuine touch with them. Some single adults come to the conclusion that the person they have been dating has little or no feelings. Many males are troubled by new attitudes that demand they be in touch with their feelings.

Mike, a young widower in my grief program, cried freely. When I complimented him on being in touch with his emotions, he responded, "I want to deal with this now, not fifteen years from now." A wise man.

Take some time to be with your feelings. They are God-given and God-blessed. Scripture says the greatest single adult who ever lived "was touched *by the feelings of* our infirmities" (Heb. 4:15, emphasis added). I have long appreciated the passage in John's Gospel when Jesus, so shaken by His friend Lazarus' death, "began to cry" (John 11:35, CEV). If Jesus can cry, I can cry.

Do everyone (and yourself) a favor: get in touch with your feelings.

This single adult had feelings and emotions and knew how to stir feelings in others. He once wrote, "You can scarcely believe what an empty, sad life I have had for the past two years." He began to lose his hearing in the late 1790s, and by 1800 his personality had been impacted, and he became more irritable and suspicious. However, his loss of hearing did not impact his composing; deep within his heart he heard such awesome music.

_____'s greatest works include the third (*Eroica*), fifth, sixth, and ninth (*Pastorale*) symphonies, the opera *Fidelio*, and his religious composition, *Missa solemnis*. Many single adults have been moved in worship as they sang his, "Ode to Joy" or "Joyful, Joyful, We Adore Thee." Who was this single adult?[1]

"Those who do not know how to weep with their whole heart do not know how to laugh either."
—*Golda Meir*[2]

24 Sink Your Roots Deep into a Community

One of the negative labels commonly but unfairly put on single adults is "uncommitted." While that label applies to some single adults, it is merely a stereotype. A positive singleness requires a sense of belonging. Healthy single adults are joiners, investing their lives in churches, neighborhoods, and civic organizations. Many such organizations thrive because of the enthusiasm single adults bring and the number of hours they are willing to invest.

Where do you belong? Where can you give of yourself and be part of making a difference? As we grow older, this becomes a crucial life question to be answered.

Successful singleness is rooted in a spiritual life, and a spiritual life requires a spiritual community. So make sure you are deeply involved in your spiritual community.

These single adults made a commitment to a dream—Texas independence. In a mission in south Texas, a group of deeply committed men crossed a line drawn in the sand by the commander, a single adult, _____ and said, "we will stay and fight with you." On February 24, 1836, a message was sent calling for assistance. This single adult was a determined realist. He concluded his appeal, "If this call is neglected, I am determined to sustain myself as long as possible and die like a soldier who never forgets what is due his own honor and that of his country. Victory or Death."

One hundred eighty-nine men, many of them single adults who had come to Texas for a new start, died at the Alamo on March 6, 1836. Their courage ensured ultimately Texas would be free. Read the names of some who have not become as famous as Crockett and Bowie.[1]

John J. Ballentine	Joseph Bayliss
Samuel Blair	Robert Brown
William R. Carey	Robert Cunningham
Charles Despallier	John Flanders
John Hubbard Forsyth	James Kenny
Jonathan L. Lindley	Thomas R. Miller
Richardson Perry	A. Spain Summerlin
Damicio Xinenes	Charles Zanco

> "It is when we have come to the end of our own resources, or rather, come to see that we never had any at all, that we are willing to accept the fact that we can do nothing and to let God do everything for us."
> —Francis Ridley Havergal[2]

25

Ask Before Buying: Do I Really Need This?

Mallitis. Have you ever had it? It is the strange malady that sends us racing to the nearest mall. Some call it "the shopping demon."

Have you ever found yourself buying things you don't really need just for the euphoria you feel while shopping? Have you ever been afraid to open a closet for fear of an avalanche? If you buy it, you've got to put it somewhere. Plastic money and credit cards only compound the problem. For some of us, the fear of being alone is temporarily deadened or dulled by browsing or buying, but there is always a price to pay in the end.

My friend, Leon Doane, taught me the difference between two words that create confusion for many of us: *want* and *need*. Contrary to popular opinion, they are not synonyms.

Shopping can become an addiction if you aren't careful. Here's a good question: Are you comfortable with your current bank balance, savings balance, and with the current debt on your credit cards? If not, practice asking yourself before making a purchase: "Do ... I ... really ... need ... this?

This single adult concluded school-teaching wasn't his future, so he saved money to buy a novelty store, and later, a toy and novelty wholesale business. _____ made a decision to finance his company's expansion through profits rather than debt. After carefully assessing the needs of the buying public, he decided to open a "five and ten" store, meaning everything sold cost less than 10 cents. How could he make any money? By buying directly from the manufacturers in large volume.

At age thirty-eight he owned fifty-one stores and grossed $3 million, a fortune by that day's standard. He developed plans for uniform operation of the stores and was one of the first to organize management training programs. The concept of "chain" stores was heavily influenced by this single adult. Who was he?[1]

> "I made my resolution (and have been enabled to keep it ever since) to show economy to myself, liberality to friends, (and) generosity to the poor."
>
> —Charles Simeon[2]

26 Treat a Senior Single Adult to a Meal

My writing career took a decisive turn after I took a senior adult to brunch in Old Town in San Diego. I was then a struggling would-be author, frustrated about how honest I should be about my divorce in *Jason Loves Jane but They Got a Divorce*. Betty listened to my frustrations, and then, with a wisdom only the years could teach, she said, "Tell the story. Don't leave out a thing." That book's publication led to my resigning an academic post and going into single adult ministry full-time.

Some younger singles do an aerial reconnaissance before they commit to a group. They stand in the back of the room and carefully analyze its membership for gray hair, white hair, and no hair. Older single adults who have been around the track a few laps have some things they could teach us, if we have teachable spirits.

Some Sunday, ask a senior single adult to a dutch brunch, or have them in your home for a snack or dessert and coffee and lots of conversation. Get to know them. Your brunch or lunch may not be as life changing as mine with Betty was, but it could lead you to a new and significant friendship.

If any single adult ever had the gift of hospitality, this New Mexico rancher did. The name _____ and his brand "Jingle-bob" stood for quality in the cattle business. At his peak he had the widest range—one-fifth of New Mexico—and the largest herds of cattle in the world; by 1875 it was estimated he had seventy to eighty thousand head of cattle on his ranch. Yet, he was known for his table. His home, Long House, could match anything in the East. Anyone who came along—friend or stranger, immigrants on the way to California, criminals fleeing a posse, a posse chasing a thief—were all welcome at the big table in his dining room, which seated twenty-six people. Three times a day he and his guests gathered for meals, and there was rarely an empty seat at any meal. His biographer observed, "Under his roof all men were equals, fellow humans on their stubbornly long or suddenly brief journeys to their own individual destinies." In the days of the wild West, although he carried a gun and large amounts of money, the only thing he ever shot was rattlesnakes. Who was this single adult?[1]

"Love never has to wait for an opportunity to demonstrate itself."
—Henrietta Mears[2]

27 Celebrate A "Lite" Christmas

What would Christmas be like with the world's craggiest bachelor, Ebenezer Scrooge? Like Scrooge, many single adults have real difficulty with the period from Thanksgiving to New Year's. Three back-to-back "family" holidays require incredible survival skills. No wonder some singles want to go into hibernation right after the Thanksgiving feast and wake up around January 4.

For some single adults, Christmas is an emotional and financial nightmare, especially for those who are experiencing their first "solo" Christmas. Our culture has taken a sacred holiday and turned it into an eating, drinking, partying, spending frenzy.

Maybe this is the year for a "lite" Christmas, a season to rediscover the real meaning of Christmas. Never forget the holidays have been impacted by singles. Single adults have given us music such as "O Little Town of Bethlehem," "Joy to the World," "It Came upon the Midnight Clear," and *Messiah*. Single adults were the first to design department store windows, often volunteering to work after the stores closed, since they did not have to rush home to families. Mistletoe was hung over doorways for young single women to be kissed, with a white berry to be plucked after every kiss (many singles insisted on mistletoe with lots of berries).[1]

In the mid-1800s, there was a tradition among German immigrant bachelors and old maids that if they needed anything in the month or two before Christmas, they waited until mid-December, bought the item with great secrecy, wrapped it, and then "gave themselves a great surprise by their unexpected and beautiful present."[2] Maybe that would be a good practice to revive.

There had long been a curiosity about Santa Claus' marital status until a single adult cleared up the question in 1899. A poet, _____, declared in her book *Goody Santa Claus on a Sleigh Ride*, the corpulent merry one from the North Pole was indeed married. A graduate of Oxford, she taught at Wellesley; in 1893, on a tour of Colorado with a group of single adults, she hiked the mountains and soaked in the beauty. One night when she could not sleep, she took a pencil and wrote these classic words, "O beautiful for spacious skies, for amber waves of grain." For two years she carried the words in her purse. Her poem, "America, the Beautiful," was first published in 1895, set to music in 1912, and is still a patriotic favorite. Who was this single adult?[3]

> *"Bah humbug!"*
> —Scrooge, before the dream
>
> *"I will honor Christmas in my heart, and try to keep it all the year. I will live in the past, the present, and the future."*
> —Scrooge, after the dream[4]

28 Give Away "Stuff" to Good Causes

Have you ever been afraid to open a closet in your house/apartment/condo for fear of an avalanche? It's amazing how much stuff we accumulate. Do you have boxes you haven't opened since the last time you moved? Have you ever moved because you need more room for all your stuff?

You could give some of that stuff away. There are good charities that will come to your door and pick it up. Maybe the teens in your church are raising money for a special project and need things for their rummage sale or auction. Do you have things you don't need or want that might be useful for their sale? It's often tempting to organize a garage sale for a little cash, but sometimes we miss the blessing in saying, "Take this." Or you might have single friends who could use a couple of items to make their homes a little more comfortable. We need to say more often, "I want you to have this."

Remember, if you keep it, you'll have to wax it or polish it or store it or clean it or vacuum it or whatever it. Give it away, and it becomes someone else's responsibility.

This single adult was a gifted linguist, speaking Italian, German, French, and English and knowledgeable in Hebrew, Greek, and Latin. She taught Sunday School and singing in her church and had memorized the Gospels, the Epistles, the Psalms, Isaiah, and the Book of Revelation. She wrote over 140 hymns, but she is best known for "Take My Life and Let It Be, Consecrated, Lord, to Thee." The third verse evoked criticism: "Take my silver and my gold, not a mite would I withhold." Such thoughts were unrealistic. Hardly, _____ responded. "We are to spend what is really needful on ourselves but not for ourselves." This single adult had donated most of her jewelry to be sold and the proceeds donated to a missionary group. She and her sister raided the "rubbish drawers" of their friends to find items to use in tidying up children for Sunday School. She also collected scraps of carpet, old curtains, to help make poor cottages of impoverished villagers more comfortable. Who was this single adult?[1]

> "There must be a great new conception of our stewardship to God if we would have fellowship with him in our service. Money is one of his all-powerful agencies, but without ourselves, our love, our time, money may be made into a curse, not a blessing. All things are possible with God, but it is only through man, through the Church, that God can do the impossible things for humanity."
>
> —Belle Bennett[2]

29 Read Historical Markers

Although I have a degree in history, for years I have jogged by a historical marker at 78th and Holmes and never paid much attention. The other day I stopped and was stunned to discover a Civil War battle took place in my neighborhood. When we hear "Civil War," we usually think of Virginia or Tennessee, not Kansas City! Yet on October 22, 1864, a group of Confederates tried to overrun a Yankee defense line on Thomas Mockbee's farm (my neighborhood), and a battle broke out. When the smoke cleared, thirty men had died and fififty-two had been wounded. I had not known a slice of history took place in my own backyard.

Next time you pass a historical marker, slow down. Remember, historical markers represent the lives of people like yourself, people who enjoyed life as you do. Take time to honor them as you pass a historical marker.

These two single adults made a difference through distributing the money they made as enthusiastic businessmen.

_____ left school when he was twelve and went to work for his uncle; however, they had a falling-out when the young man fell in love with his cousin and the uncle did not approve. The single man remained a lifelong bachelor. His first year in his own business he made $200,000, a small fortune in those days. Soon he began building warehouses and went into the banking and insurance business. This single was the largest stockholder of the Baltimore and Ohio Railroad. Concerned by the cholera and yellow fever epidemics, he gave $7 million in 1870 to found this nation's first research university as well as a great hospital with an innovative program in nurses' training.

_____ made his money early in trading and quickly branched into buying and selling New Orleans' real estate. He predicted the demise of slavery in the South and its economic consequences. He was frugal, industrious, tenacious,

"exacting to the last penny." He had a generous heart and shared his wealth with churches, schools, and charities. In 1882 he made his first major donation—all his New Orleans real estate and a sizable amount of cash—to what was then called the University of Louisiana; he would have given more, but he died without a will. The university went private and was renamed for its benefactor.

Who were these two single adults who have universities named after them?[1]

> "If a man does not keep pace with his companions, perhaps it is because he hears a different drummer. Let him step to the music he hears, however measured or far away."
>
> —Henry David Thoreau[2]

30 Make the Most of Sundays

There was a time in my childhood—and I'm not that old!—when no businesses were open on Sundays. People went to church; those who didn't stayed home then. Slowly across the years, Sunday has become just another day. "Remember the Sabbath day" seems archaic, especially in a culture that prizes workaholism. No wonder we're tired. We've ignored a Commandment and a God-modeled principle. Genesis reports, "So on the seventh day He rested from all His work" (2:2). After the work of creation, God needed a break.

Moreover, "God blessed the seventh day and made it holy, because on it He rested from all the work of creating that He had done" (v. 3). If God needed rest, how much more do we?

Admittedly, some of us cannot observe Sunday as our day of rest or our Sabbath. We can honor our day off and make it "holy" by setting aside a quiet time, listening to hymns or praise songs, by watching a video of a Sunday worship service, or simply by ensuring a large chunk of our day off is spent resting.

Sad to say, many Christians do not have, and could not recognize, a true Sabbath. Sunday is the day to do everything that didn't get done in the previous week or to prepare for the week ahead. Many of us start Monday tired from a busy, overscheduled weekend.

Single adults sometimes make bad decisions because they are physically exhausted. More make bad decisions because they do not have a Sabbath. One popular restaurant chain reminds us, "You deserve a break today." Well, God says, "You deserve a break this week. . . . Try a Sabbath!"

Although this single could have had her choice of suitors, she committed her life to making a difference and never married. Her motto was, "Yes, Lord, I'll do it!" Through her appointment to the selection committee for Methodist missionaries, _____ became concerned about the practice of sending young single women to mission fields without adequate preparation. This single adult helped institute high standards, founded Scarritt College to provide such training, and raised large amounts of money to support the effort. She was known for her strict observance of the Sabbath. She often would travel as far as she could on Saturday, then stop and wait until Monday to resume. On one layover in Birmingham, she had opportunity to learn about the steel mills. As a result of what she saw, she helped organize a series of community centers to reach these workers. Who was this single adult?[1]

> "How shall I ever be able to thank God sufficiently?"
> —Søren Kierkegaard[2]

31 Go Back to School

For a growing number of adults, September means "going back to school." College is no longer the exclusive domain of twenty-year-olds. The number of adults age thirty-five and over enrolled in college programs has increased 96 percent over the past decade. Yes, it can be a challenge to hold down a full-time job and work on completing a degree, but it could be the key to your economic future, since the workplace puts a premium on education and training. Moreover, many single adults are going back to school in a new area to expand their horizons or because they want to give some attention to areas such as the humanities that didn't get their full attention the first go-around.

Betty Ann Potter, a single adult, entered the University of Missouri at age sixty, lived in the dorm, and four years later completed her B.A. in travel/tourism with a 4.0.[1]

Other singles are going back to take "fun" courses. Next September might be the time for you to go back to school.

As a young single adult, she opened a school for black children in Wilmington, Delaware, in 1840, and later taught in New York. Following the passage of the Fugitive Slave Law in 1850, she, along with many free blacks, moved to Canada. She became a strong advocate of black immigration to Canada and became the first black female to develop a strong data base to use for propaganda purposes.

She wrote "Notes on Canada West" to counteract the ugly stories about life for blacks in Canada being circulated by southern slave owners. She became a single parent after her husband of four years died in 1860.

During the Civil War she recruited troops for the Union Army. After the war she opened a school for black children in Washington and went back to school, becoming the first black woman lawyer in this country, graduating from Howard University in 1870 at age forty-seven. _____ opened her law office in Washington and became one of the few women to vote in federal elections during Reconstruction. Who was this single adult?[2]

"Our doubts are traitors
And make us lose the good we oft
    might win
By fearing to attempt."
—Sarah Josepha Hale[3]

32 Enjoy, Explore, Protect Nature

Many Sundays I have sung with the congregation, "This Is My Father's World" and have been captured by the words, "Of rocks and trees, of skies and seas; His hand the wonders wrought." Genesis says man was placed in the Garden "to work and to take care of it." Kentucky farmer/poet Wendell Berry observes, Christians "have lately shown little inclination to honor the earth or to protect it from those who would dishonor it."[1]

Yet, earth is not our playground; it is our "fragile" home. Berry says, "The ecological teaching of the Bible is simply inescapable: God made the world because He wanted it made. He thinks the world is good, and He loves it (enough to send His Son to die for it). It is His world; He has never relinquished His title to it. He has never revoked the conditions . . . that oblige us to take excellent care of it."[2]

When I go to the health club, I drive along a section of the Little Blue River. Hundreds of years ago Indians swam in and fished from it. Settlers watered their stock there en route to Oregon; more recently, on hot summer days boys sneaked away from their chores and dived into its cool greenness. Today, you can't fish in it and no one would put a toe into it. It is polluted from industrial wastes. This aspect of God's creation has been abused, but before that it was taken for granted. What are you doing as a single adult to enjoy, explore, and protect nature?

"A few thousand words" from this single adult and the world took a different direction. *Silent Spring*, her book on the dangers of the use of DDT, was the best-seller that launched the environmental movement. She survived discrimination when she decided to study science at Johns Hopkins. After graduation, she became one of the first women ever hired by the U.S. Bureau of Fisheries. Soon thereafter, she became a single parent when her older sister died and this young scientist took in her two small girls.

_____'s early writing, *The Sea Around Us*, was assumed to have been written by a man because of its technical excellence. The *New York Times* honored it as the most outstanding book of the year. At age fifty, she became a single parent again when she adopted her great nephew after his mother's death. She hoped the "ugly facts" in her books would not distract the readers from understanding "the beauty of the living world I was trying to save." Who was this single adult scientist?[3]

> "There are no other Everglades in the world. We simply must save the Everglades. We simply have no other choice."
>
> —Marjory Stoneman Douglas[4]

33 Respect Your Body

We hear a lot about abuse these days but not a lot about "body" abuse. Many single adults faithfully drag themselves to the gym/health club for their torture routines, grumbling, "No pain, no gain!" We live in a culture obsessed with the body. Many single adults just know that if only their _____ were _____, then they would be married!

Christian tradition teaches the body is the temple of the Holy Spirit. Therefore, the body should be reverenced but never idolized. One blessing of aging is we can finally come to terms with physiological reality. It is what is on the inside that really counts.

Respect your body by watching what and when you eat. Don't try to anesthetize yourself during a dateless evening by pigging out on junk food. Eat smart.

Respect your body by getting enough sleep and exercise. Join a health club if it fits into your budget, but never forget that walking is profitable as well as inexpensive. Get plenty of sleep. Treat yourself to naps and "sleep in." The old adage, "Early to bed, early to rise, makes a [single] healthy, wealthy, and wise," may be stretching it a bit, but good sleep patterns will make you a better person to be around. A lot of bad decisions are made by tired singles. Remember, there may be transplants for individual body parts, but there is no total body transplant.

Bodies can change; this single adult learned that reality in Vietnam when he lost both legs and his right arm in a grenade explosion a month before he was to return home. No one expected him to live, but _____ had grown up reading the Bible, and in his hour of need, he remembered Paul's words, "Glory in tribulations, knowing that tribulations produces perseverance; and perseverance, character; and character, hope. And hope does not disappoint us" (Rom. 5:3–5).

This single adult served two terms in the Georgia legislature, lost a race for lieutenant governor, and then joined the permanent staff of the U.S. Senate Committee on Veterans' Affairs. In 1976, President Carter appointed him Director of Veterans Affairs, the youngest man ever to run the agency, responding to the needs of six million veterans.

Since 1982, he has served as Georgia's Secretary of State. He explained his reaction to his body, "Life doesn't revolve around an arm and a leg. People look at you the way you look at yourself." He told one reporter, "I want to put my best foot forward, even though it is plastic." Who is this single adult?[1]

> *"I'm living one day at a time. These bodies of ours are only something God gives us to tote ourselves around in. It's the spirit that counts."*
> —Martha Berry[2]

34 Laugh . . . Tell Jokes

When Norman Cousins was diagnosed with a fatal disease, he refused to accept that as reality. Instead, he checked into a hospital with a stack of joke books and comedy videos. He recovered and insists his healing happened because he learned to laugh.

Our lives are much more pleasant if we look for humor along the way. Keep some humorous books in your personal library. Try to avoid books that laugh at people rather than laughing with them.

Today, your assignment is to laugh. Go to the video store and rent some Abbott and Costello, Marx Brothers, or Three Stooges flicks and pop some popcorn and laugh.

OK, I'll try one joke. Did you hear about the old maid who died and left a will stipulating that she have female pallbearers? She said, "If no man took me out while I was alive, six men are not going to take me out after I'm dead!"

Now, it's your turn. Tell someone a joke.

In 1884 the Democrats were pleased; the White House would be theirs again for the first time in a quarter century. The reform governor of New York, a bachelor, was sure to be elected. _____ who had been a district attorney county sheriff and reform mayor of Buffalo, was an ideal candidate.

On July 21, newspapers carried the story that he had fathered a son out of wedlock. Democratic politicians looked for some way to manage the story for the least political damage. "Say it ain't so" they pleaded. The candidate answered with three words that shocked the experts and the American people as well: "Tell the truth." Yes, he had fathered the child, but he had financially cared for his son and the boy's mother.

On election day, he won by a scant twenty-three thousand votes; once in office, he totally revamped the political patronage system. On June 2, 1886, he stunned the nation by marrying Francis Folsom in the first presidential wedding in the White House. Who was he?[1]

> "Whatever the alternatives, we can sprinkle humor over them."
> —Elva McAllaster[2]

35 Visit Cemeteries

OK, before you get hostile, go in daylight hours. A walk through a cemetery pushes us to confront one of life's central realities—we are going to die.

I often eat lunch in a large beautiful cemetery near my home. I have gone there when I needed a place to think, to wrestle with some difficult decision. A widow in one of my conferences said she learned to drive in a cemetery, "Like who was I going to hurt?!" she added.

I like to visit the graves of famous single adults. I got ejected from a London cemetery for singing at the grave of hymnist Isaac Watts. "This is no place for singing!" the caretaker announced. "But he wrote the song!" I protested. "I don't care if the Queen Mum herself wrote it. We aren't having any singing!" Maybe this suggestion isn't for everyone, but try it. At least once.

I spent two hours trying to find the grave of this single adult in Hong Kong. God said to her: "I want you." By October 1920, _____ was in China where she easily learned the languages and dialects. Despite the turmoil in China, she traveled alone, noting, "While souls are dying, one cannot afford to wait for more peaceful times." She adopted the Chinese life-style and wardrobe and, eventually, Chinese children. As war came to the Far East, the Mission Board ordered her to leave, but she stayed, saying, "No one in the States needs me; the Chinese do. I'm staying."

Finally, after China became Communist, she left. In 1956 she was appointed to Taiwan but decided after a brief stop in Hong Kong to go no further. She launched a new mission work nine miles from the Mainland China border.

When she reached mandatory retirement age, she refused to return home saying, "Missionaries do not retire; missionaries die."

As I searched for her grave one hot August afternoon, a cemetery worker had compassion on me and took me to the cemetery office. He dialed a number, spoke rapidly, and handed the phone to me. A voice asked in broken English,

"Who you want?"

"_____," I answered slowly, then spelled the last name.

"The Christian?" the voice asked. I felt as if the wind had been knocked out of me. "Put worker on phone!" the voice snapped. Minutes later I stood at her grave. Although she had died in 1966, twenty-two years later she was still known in Hong Kong as "The Christian." What a testimony! Who was this single adult?[1]

"Let me read with open eyes the book my days are writing—and learn."

—Dag Hammarsjkold

*"For him who has faith,
The last miracle
Shall be greater than the first."*

—Dag Hammarsjkold[2]

---

36 Forgive!

Too many people walk around with a backpack jammed full with wounds, hurts, slights, wrongs, and unfairnesses. After five minutes with them you are looking for an exit. Many of them think forgiveness is an emotion. They think one of these days they'll get around to forgiving the people who have hurt them.

No, forgiveness is a decision. I choose to forgive or not to forgive. Either decision has consequences. Unforgiveness poisons the soil of the soul so the seeds of relationship cannot grow. Too many of us cling to fantasies of the offender coming crawling back on hands and knees to beg our forgiveness. Some of us rehearse our lines with plans to settle the score. What a tragedy! Do yourself a big favor: forgive.

Many people called this young single adult nurse "the poor man's Florence Nightingale." She opened a school of nursing in Belgium, challenging the tradition that nurses had to be nuns. She witnessed the horrors of World War I, caring for the mangled bodies of soldiers brought to her hospital. _____ bravely spoke out against the brutalities of war. Although she was warned that expressing such opinions could endanger her life, she refused to be silenced. "There is," she countered, "a higher duty than prudence."

On October 8, 1915, she and thirty-three other nurses were tried for helping French soldiers escape from her hospital. In court she admitted her involvement, explaining, "It was my duty to save lives."

As she was led to the firing line, she said,"I have no fear nor shirking. I have seen death so often it is not strange or fearful to me. I expected it would end like this. I thank God for this ten weeks' quiet before the end. They have all been very kind to me here. But this I would say, standing as I do in view of God and eternity. I realize that patriotism is not enough. I must have no hatred or bitterness toward anyone." That included the men who made up the firing squad that shot her to death on October 12, 1915.[1] Who was she?

> "The wisest plan is to let by-gones be by-gones."
> —R.E.B. Baylor[2]

37 Say "I'm Sorry"

I have long believed ten words could eliminate most of the problems of talk shows' guests. "I am sorry," "I was wrong," and "Will you forgive me?" A lot of single adults carry the excess emotional baggage of "He said/she said/I should have said . . ." While it's useless to cry over spilled milk, you can make amends. Sometimes we do say "I'm sorry" but in such a way as to indict the listener, "But it was your fault that I lost my temper." Some things cannot be as they were; often, they can be better. I have to be willing to make the first move toward reconciliation.

Life took a turn for this single adult when a group of students met under a haystack to pray for the unsaved in foreign lands. Five of the students felt called to volunteer for mission service. After negotiations with the London Missionary Society, this single adult found himself all but excluded because he had not finished seminary, had no money, and had not resolved a relationship with Rebecca Eaton, to whom he had proposed without telling her about his call to missions.

Then the American Board of Commissioners for Foreign Missions agreed to send him if he could raise his own money. In February 1812 he was commissioned and soon found himself en route to India. However, when he reached India he was baptized by Baptist missionaries and had to return home to explain his theological shift to his sending agency.

_____ planned to return to the mission field but became involved in the founding of a nationwide Baptist society to support foreign missions.

He founded Columbian College in Washington, D.C. in 1820, but his vision exceeded financial reality. In 1825 this single adult was terminated as agent or chief fund raiser.

He said, "I'm sorry" and spent the rest of his life raising money to pay off the debts of what eventually became George Washington University. This single adult was influential in the founding of Georgetown College, Wake Forest University, Furman University, and the University of Richmond. Who was he?[1]

> "It was as if I had worked for years on the wrong side of a tapestry, learning accurately all its lines and figures, and yet always missing its color and sheen."
>
> —Anna Louise Strong [2]

38 Park Farther out in Parking Lots

Why is it that when we're in a hurry we can't find a decent parking space? Why do so many of us get upset because someone takes a space we wanted or because we have to take a space out on the edge of the parking lot?

I think you can learn a lot about people by riding with them while they are looking for a parking space. Most people get tense or frustrated or even angry. Do you know where I get the most frustrated over not finding a space right at the door? The health club. I know, it doesn't make sense.

After all, I went there to get my exercise....

Most of us do *need* the exercise

Next time you can't find a space as close as you want, relax. Why not try taking the first space you find. You might even get to the store more quickly than if you circled and circled and circled.

We might still be walking if it had not been for the vision of two single adult brothers who owned a bicycle shop in Dayton, Ohio, but kept reading everything they could find on aeronautics.

They built the nation's first wind tunnel and an engine for a "heavier-than-air" craft. On December 17, 1903, they made history when one brother flew 120 feet in 12 seconds. Later, the other brother flew 852 feet in 59 seconds.

In 1906, _____ and_____ got their patents and soon signed a contract with the War Department to build a plane that could fly forty miles-per-hour.

Who were these amazing single adults?[1]

> *"But God does not expect the impossible from us; He only expects us to expect the impossible from Him."*
> —*Eugenia Price*[2]

39 Treasure Your Uniqueness

Take a moment to look at your fingerprints. No one has fingerprints like yours. They are unique, yet we live in a culture that stresses uniformity and conformity, the need to fit in.

I love what Robert Fulghum said in *Maybe, Maybe Not*, "Sometimes history knocks at the most ordinary door to see if anyone is at home. Sometimes someone is."[1] We have been uniquely gifted, uniquely created, and uniquely enabled; yet, some of us are waiting for only one knock on our door—the impatient rap of the right mate. Sadly, it's easier to covet our neighbor's uniqueness. The Ten Commandments tell us not to covet our neighbor's house or wife or oxen or donkeys (and since no one in my neighborhood has the latter, I don't have to worry). Yet, there is the last phrase, "or anything that belongs to your neighbor" (Ex. 20:17) which I assume means intangibles like my neighbor's uniqueness.

Do yourself a favor: treasure your uniqueness.

When this single adult was nominated to become the 105th justice of the United States Supreme Court following the bitter defeat of Robert Bork, many senators and much of the media didn't know what to do with his uniqueness. _____ had impressive credentials: Harvard Law School, Rhodes Scholar at Oxford, Attorney General of New Hampshire, State Supreme Court Justice, and member of the U.S. Court of Appeals, First Circuit. When he arrived in Washington to face the Senate Judiciary Committee, more focus was on the bachelor from the Granite State than the jurist. One headline screamed, "Bachelorhood an Unspoken Issue for Court Nominee."

He was easily confirmed, however, by the Senate ninety to nine and took his seat on the court in October 1990.

After his first weeks on the court, when asked about his experience, he said, "It's a lot of work. I'm trying to earn my salary" which ironically, he was unaware of when he signed the lease for his spartan bachelor digs near the court. Who is this single adult?[2]

> "It is difficult for some to acknowledge the beauty and dignity of singleness as such. They may even go so far as to regard being single as a kind of curse, an alienating condition. . . . Does it not occur to us that God may have made Adam lone and unique exactly to express the profound mystery of our original, never-to-be-duplicated, human formation? He first did create one person in celebration of uniqueness; only then did He give this person a mate in celebration of togetherness. Out of solitude came the quest for solidarity, and not the other way around. Try as we may, we cannot reason our way out of original aloneness. Uniqueness precedes union once we leave our mother's womb."
>
> —Susan Muto[3]

40 Be a Secret Robin Hood

Several years ago, I was impressed by a group of anonymous single adults who formed a group called "Robin Hoods of Los Angeles" and took it upon themselves to do random acts of kindness, often for other single adults.

A single parent had been driving on "bald" tires. One Sunday at her church, an usher told her that her car was blocking someone. "I'll move it," she said quickly. "Oh, no, just give me the keys." She did.

When she emerged from the worship service a couple of hours later, she discovered four brand new tires and a spare. A note on the windshield said, "Robin Hoods of Los Angeles."

Maybe you've seen the bumper sticker, "Practice random kindness and senseless acts of beauty." Be sensitive. Listen to soft-spoken or unspoken needs. Form a merry band of singles and find acts of kindness to do. And keep it a secret.

This single adult revolutionized the world with his innovations in explosives, particularly nitroglycerin and dynamite, which he originally thought would be used in mines and quarries. By age forty _____ was one of the richest men in the world. Ironically, his biographer called him "the loneliest man in the world." His mother was always his confidante; he never married because the woman he loved was from a socially unacceptable family.

When his brother Ludwig died, as this single adult read the obituary in the newspaper, he was stunned to discover the reporter had confused the two brothers and that the obituary was actually his own rather than his brother's. He was stunned to read that he was "the merchant of death." He vowed he would not be remembered this way, so he established a fund to award annual prizes in literature, medicine, chemistry, physics, and the encouragement of peace. He concluded, "I have a more and more earnest wish to see a red-rose peace sprout in this explosive world." Ironic words from a man who provided the resources to make it so explosive. Who was this single adult?[1]

> "I have been too anxious to do great things. The lust [for] praise has ever been my besetting sin."
> —Robert Murray McCheyne[2]

41 Travel

When I grew up, we never went on vacations and all those "Having a great time . . . wish you were here!" cards really rankled me. Today I send the postcards. As my friend Albin Whitworth says, "Why stay home when you can go somewhere?"

I've been to Westminster Abbey and the Great Wall of China. I've eaten Kentucky Fried Chicken in Peking and at McDonald's in Hong Kong. I've climbed all six hundred plus steps to the top of St. Peter's and I've ridden camels in Cairo. I've sung with the choir at Canterbury Cathedral, and I've been to John Wesley's grave in London and Lottie Moon's home in China.

My worldview has been stretched because I have spent two Thanksgivings I will never forget in Haiti (one during a coup) and because I have been to what used to be Yugoslavia. When I see pictures from those areas on TV or in the paper, I have to pause: I've been there; I have friends there.

There are also things within thirty miles of my home that tourists come to snap photos of—places that I have never seen. I bet the same is true with you. It's ironic that we travel halfway around the world and ignore our own backyard.

So, do a local vacation. Dress up as a tourist and spend your vacation exploring the local tourist sites.

Ill health and curiosity sent this single adult from Independence, Missouri, westward in 1831, headed for Santa Fe. During the long, hazardous trek, his health improved and he decided to become a trader, making nine westward expeditions. His curiosity led him to make copious notes of all that caught his eye. His notes led to his book *Commerce of the Prairies*, published in 1844. The book was an instant success.

In 1846 he rode twelve hundred miles on horseback to join the young patriots at San Antonio, and he fought in Mexico.

In 1849 the call to California was too great to pass up, so he headed for the mines of Northern California. He died of hunger and exposure in 1850. His book, which established him as the historian of Santa Fe trade, is considered a classic on the frontier and tempted many people to go West. Who was this single adult?[1]

On Why She Never Married

"I'm not really the marrying kind. And may I say very frankly that you can do without sex, too . . . When you're interested in doing things, sex is not so important, and besides, you have a lot more energy to put into what you want to do."

—Marjorie Stoneman Douglas[2]

42 Send Lots of Greeting Cards

One bright card came the other day, "When you reach the end of the road, there's only one thing to do: Build More Road!" Cards are a way of saying, "I care" or "I am concerned." For those moments when we do not have the "right" words at our disposal, cards can say them for us. You may prefer cards with blank insides, which allow you to be creative or mushy or gushy.

Send cards. Send lots of cards. For the price of a postage stamp you can make somebody's day.

What to do with the cards you receive? Keep them. I have a large basketful in my living room. I can reach in and reread and reenjoy the card. Some are even better the second time. I also pray for the senders of the cards in that basket. You can use cards as bookmarks. Some can be recycled: cut off the front and you have a postcard. Your card could make the difference in someone's day.

Know why you haven't had diphtheria? Because of a single adult whose world changed when she looked into a microscope for the first time. When her niece died, this single adult wondered why doctors could not have done more.

In 1887, she decided to attend medical school (over her mother's objections until the young woman said she *might* become a medical missionary), graduating in 1891. Three years later she began working in the New York City Department of Health's diagnostic lab, investigating an antitoxin for diphtheria, then a leading cause of childhood death. In 1894, _____ had a major breakthrough, discovering what came to be called Park-Williams #8, a substance still in use in producing toxin today. As a result of her efforts, diphtheria became increasingly rare in most of the Western world. She was also heavily involved in disease control in the military during World War II. She used her influence to advance the cause of women in medicine. Who was this single adult?[1]

WHY I NEVER MARRIED...

"It's just that I never found a man who can cook."

—Virginia Apgar[2]

---

43 Teach a Bible Study Class

"Me? Teach a Bible study class? You've got to be kidding!"

No one said that you had to be able to preach like Billy Graham. Teaching is an opportunity to get involved in the lives of others. What greater gift could you give someone than to help them deepen their faith and appreciation of Scripture?

It will take preparation, but you are rewarded with a growing knowledge of Scripture. You have an opportunity to see your pupils grow in their knowledge and faith. Besides, someone taught you. Look at the impact teachers have had on you. Now is a good time to pay back some of that debt we owe.

In March 1841 a Harvard Divinity School student asked _____ to substitute teach his Sunday School class for women at the Cambridge jail. This single adult had been snubbed by the elite of Boston society, had had an engagement broken, but she agreed to the request.

That first Sunday floored her. She found foul, bare, unheated quarters for the women and little privacy. She discovered that the insane were housed with drunks, vagrants, prostitutes and hardened criminals. She found naked men chained to stakes. When she protested, she was told, "Crazy folks don't feel the cold." "If I am cold," she declared, "they are cold! Get them some heat!"

She launched an eighteen-month investigation into the care of the mentally ill that shocked the state government into action. Little did she know that volunteering to teach a Sunday School class would revolutionize her life.

When the Civil War broke out, she volunteered for service, and on June 10, 1861, she was appointed superintendent of nurses for the Union Army. When the President asked her how she managed to get so much done, she answered, "God requires no more to be accomplished than He gives time for performing." Who was this single adult?[1]

> "I wish I were able to give you some wonderful reports to encourage you, but our work is so different from most works. It takes a lifetime for one of my babies to grow up and become important, if ever . . . Books may be destroyed, papers may be burned or lost, but the seeds planted in the heart of a child may lie dormant for years and then suddenly spring into life."
>
> —Lillian Thrasher[2]

44

Get out of Debt

One of the fastest growing addictions in this country is ironically an addiction to plastic—a little piece of plastic three inches by two inches with a long series of numbers.

In the wrong hands credit cards can be lethal. You know the routine: you're feeling a little "down," so you go to the mall. Something catches your eye, so you hand over your card, and moments later you walk out with your purchase. Days pass. One day an envelope comes and you get a sinking feeling in your stomach. You've been struck with the "First of the Month Blues."

Are you suffering from the First of the Month Blues? Are you hoping a mate with a wad of cash will come along to bail you out of your financial straits? Now is an excellent time to cut up or cancel a credit card and go to a cash system. You may feel that you'll never get out of debt, but if you go to the Credit Bureau, you will find people who can help you create a plan.

Now is a good time to get out of debt.

In 1930, during the Depression, this single adult was elected mayor of Detroit, which had more than 100,000 unemployed persons. Because he insisted that no one would go hungry, he worked incessantly to find money to meet the financial obligations and compassionate responsibilities of the city. He sharply reduced city spending and promised banks that the city would live within its income. In 1936 _____ was elected governor of Michigan. In 1939 he was appointed attorney general of the United States and worked to prosecute political corruption in municipal governments. In 1940 he was appointed to the Supreme Court, but after the attack on Pearl Harbor he attempted to resign in order to lead a combat troop. Although often criticized for his court opinions, he continually reminded the court of the phrase "justice for all." He labeled the wartime resettlement of Japanese-American citizens as racism. Who was this single adult?[1]

> "He who serves God with what costs him nothing will do very little service, you may depend on it."
> —Susan Warner[2]

45 Get to Know Single Adults in the Bible

Single adults often assume that the Christian faith is only a family-based religion; indeed, many churches are family-centric. Single adults do not fit in because they do not have a family, or, in the case of single parents, a traditional family. While Christianity has been heavily influenced by Judaism, it would be an error to assume that the Christian community has not been interested in and enhanced by single adults.

In a book I highly recommend, *Famous Singles of the Bible* (Broadman), Brain Harbour concedes, "Singleness was not a common life-style in Bible times; most people were married." However, "sprinkled throughout the Scriptures are cameos of men and women who, either by choice or circumstance, sometimes spent time in the single state."[1] The three key "shapers" of the New Testament were unmarried: John the Baptist, Jesus, and the Apostle Paul.

Who are some of the singles in the Bible? Harbour tells us about:

- *The Shunned Single: Hagar (Gen. 16:1-16; 21:1-20)*
- *The Secular Single: Tamar (Gen. 38:8)*
- *The Selective Single: Isaac (Gen. 21—24)*
- *The Swinging Single: Dinah (Gen. 34)*
- *The Sorrowful Single: Naomi (Book of Ruth)*
- *The Sterling Single: Vashti (Esther 1)*
- *The Serving Single: Anna (Luke 2:36-38)*

- *The Surprised Single:*
  The Samaritan Woman (John 4:1-42)

I would add that there are others waiting to be discovered in your reading and research. Play detective.

Although he was a brilliant Oxford mathematician, this man's future was challenged when he read the journal of David Brainerd, single adult missionary to the American Indians. Putting the book aside, he prayed, "Here I am Lord. Send me to the ends of the earth; send me to the rough, the savage pagans of the wilderness."

_____ was accepted as a candidate for the Church Mission Society of England, but had his heart broken when the woman he loved insisted that she could not marry him until her previous fiancé married or died. Engagements were taken extremely seriously in those days.

In 1805 he was appointed a chaplain with the British East Indian Trading Company and spent the next seven years in India, Persia, and Arabia, where he translated the Bible into Arabic, Persian, and Hindustani, a most remarkable accomplishment and one which paved the way for evangelism of these peoples.

He died October 16, 1812 at age thirty-one, en route to Constantinople and London. Who was this single adult?[2]

> *"If you come across something in the Scriptures that in your limited knowledge you do not understand just then, lay the item aside temporarily and go on. Later on in your study, and in your spiritual maturity, you will find the solution."*
>
> —Henrietta Mears[3]

46 Write Your Will

Don't even consider skipping this section. Many single adults do not want to think about death, so they do not have a will or funeral plans, and their family, in a time of great emotional pain, is further burdened.

Sarah thought she had her entire life ahead of her but a drunken driver hit her head-on. She died instantly. The grief-stricken family came to Kansas City and discovered few financial records. The family faced a nightmare, trying to figure out her bankcards, checkbook, and savings ac-counts. Finally, someone went through her address book and located an ac-countant who did her taxes.

What are *your* wishes? What about your friends? How is your family to know to call Joe in Portland because he would want to come to the funeral?

What about memorials? Maybe you want florists to work overtime, or may-be you'd rather mourners donate mon-ey to your chosen organization.

What about your estate? Do you want your money to help your nieces to college? If you die without a will, guess who gets to enjoy a major chunk of your estate? The government.

Planning is a vital. You may want to pick up a copy of Ron DelBene's book-let, *When You Want Your Wishes Known* (Upper Room Books). Write your will and tell someone where it can be found

This single adult's love of books was encouraged by his mother. After graduation from Harvard, he decided to make a career of collecting rare books.

_____ spent hours rummaging through old bookstores, sometimes finding literary gems. But in time he began to think about what he should do with his books. He did not wish to be remembered primarily as a collector of books, but wanted to be linked to a great collection of books in a great library.

In London, before sailing on the maiden voyage of a new ocean liner, he bought a 350-year-old copy of Bacon's *Essaies*, saying jokingly, "I think I'll take this little Bacon with me in my pocket, and if I am shipwrecked it will go with me."

On 12 April 1912, this single adult stood on the deck on the sinking *Titanic* and waved to his mother in a lifeboat; at 2:20 a.m., he went down with the ship.

Three years later Harvard opened a massive new library, a gift from a grief-stricken mother. Who was this single adult?[1]

> *"No matter how lonely you get or how many birth announcements you receive, the trick is not to get frightened. There's nothing wrong with being alone."*
>
> —Wendy Wasserstein[2]

47 Tip Well and Smile at Servers

be sensitive to the person serving you. Tip well. Smile.

You're out with a group of single adults in a restaurant. The bill comes and you see that it will take a mathematical genius to sort it out. Someone is appointed money collector and you come up a couple of dollars short. Why? Some single adults are stingy tippers. Some of us think the waiter has to "earn" or deserve the tip.

Whenever I have a meal with my single friend Ilona, she *always* prays for our food and our waiter/waitress *and* she always tips well. Next time you're in a restaurant,

Mentally ill people have not always been treated with dignity in this country; two single adults, Dorothea Dix and _____ lobbied for more compassionate care. For forty-eight years this single adult taught medical jurisprudence in some of the nation's leading medical schools. He was New York's first state commissioner of lunacy and was an early expert on insanity as a legal defense. He visited mental hospitals not to snoop but to show genuine interest in the employees, who he saw as "ministers' to the mentally compromised.

This single adult, however, had a few eccentricities that brought smiles to his colleagues. He refused to pay more than twenty-five cents for lunch, which could not have generated much of a tip. Who was this single adult?[1]

> "I long to accomplish a great and noble task, but it is my chief duty to accomplish humble tasks as though they were great and noble. The world is moved along not by the mighty shoves of its heroes, but also by the aggregate of the tiny pushes of each honest worker."
>
> —Helen Keller[2]

48 Bake

For several years I had Christmas cookie decorating parties. I baked the sugar cookies, prepared the icing and collected the decorating goodies, set up folding tables in my living room and welcomed friends over. The rule was that everyone had to decorate at least one cookie. If you messed up, you ate the cookie and started over.

Do you remember coming home from school to the smell of homemade cookies? Have you ever walked into someone's home, smelled the aroma, and heard the words, *fresh from the oven*? Personally, I am addicted to warm, moist cookies; and I probably wouldn't turn down cakes, pies, or cobblers either. Who has time to bake?

Sadly, many of us, male and female, have neglected or lost the baking skills our ancestors had. Recipes that passed from generation to generation are gradually being forgotten, especially for those of us who are at the end of the family tree.

Why not ask your mother, aunt, grandmother, or some other talented cook to show you their baking secrets. It could be a great way to spend a Saturday. Who knows, you might hear the ultimate compliment—"May I have your recipe?"

In 1920 this single adult completed the M.A. and M.R.E. at Boston University and, despite male faculty reservations, went on to complete the Ph.D. in religion in 1923. As a faculty member at Elmira College, she was a resource to many Methodist churches and wrote five books on philosophy and ethics.

Her life changed when her father, on his deathbed, urged her, "Write more about Jesus Christ." Her next thirty-three books took up that challenge. _____ joined the faculty of Garrett Theological Seminary and emphasizing her conviction that the task of theologians was "to make Christianity meaningful to the people in the pews."

Colleagues and students always enjoyed visits to her home, where they were served the "theological cookies and pies" she baked. Her warm hospitality encouraged many discouraged and tired students.[1]

On Why She Never Married:

"Politics is almost totally consuming. . . . A good marriage requires that one attend to it and not treat it as another hobby."

—Barbara Jordan[2]

---

49 Decide What You Do Makes a Difference

Ten minutes of network news can fill us with a sense of despair. Heartaches. tragedies. It would be tempting to crawl in our shells and wait for the end.

Christians do not have that right or privilege. Throughout history, in dark hours, single adults have been survivors. They know that stars are the brightest in the darkest night.

How can Christians do that? They know that they are forgiven and accepted and empowered; they dare to believe Scripture. They dare to believe that God calls each of us to make a difference; that despair is the real sin in our day.

Nancy Wood writes, "You must not be afraid to travel where there are no roads. You must not give in to the darkness when there is no sign of light."[1] There come those moments when it would be easy to throw in the towel. In those moments, we can rely on our faith, moored deeply in the riches of God's love, and go on. Sometimes, we must leave the results to time and to God.

Consider making this statement by William James a daily affirmation:

> I WILL LIVE MY LIFE
> AS THOUGH WHAT I DO
> MAKES A DIFFERENCE!

This person became a rich widow when her husband died in 1880, leaving her $20 million in cash and stocks which paid dividends of $1,250 a day. She became despondent over her husband's death and the death of her daughter, and consulted a medium who told her that her life was cursed by the ghosts of all the people who had been killed by the guns her husband's company had manufactured. She would know peace only if she would build a house for the rest of her life; if the hammering ever stopped for a moment she would die.

_____ moved to San Jose, California, and began remodeling a farmhouse. For 38 years carpenters worked around the clock, creating this country's strangest house with 10,000 windows; 2,000 doors (leading nowhere); 47 fireplaces; 40 bedrooms; 40 staircases; 6 kitchens. At one time, some historians conclude, there may have been as many as 750 rooms, but destruction was also a way to keep the hammers going.

This widow eventually spent an estimated $40 million on the house, today a museum. One has to wonder how much darkness in the world could have been banished if that money had been used more wisely, if that widow had lived as if she could make a difference. Who was this single adult with a building fixation?[2]

> *"It is not how many years we live, but how we live them."*
> —*Evangeline Booth*[3]

50 Remember Your Priorities

A friend of mine says, "The question is not, 'Is there life after death?' but 'Is there *life* during life?'" What are you doing with this precious time of your life called *now*? While I have been writing *51 Good Things*, I have said good-bye to two single friends who died far too young. Being at their deathbeds and listening to them has given me a fresh glimpse of the preciousness of life.

This single season takes on new meaning when you really listen to the words of the greatest single adult who ever lived. "I came so they can have real and eternal life, more and better life than they ever dreamed of" (John 10:10, Peterson, see chap. 16 notes, no. 2). Jesus offers you the abundant life. Now. Today. This moment.

Jesus urges us, "Seek first his kingdom and his righteousness, and all these things will be given to you as well" (Matt. 6:33). Eugene Peterson translates this command:

"Steep your life in God-reality, God-initiative, God-provisions. Don't worry about missing out. You'll find all your everyday human concerns will be met. Give all your attention to what God is doing right now, and don't get worked up about what may or may not happen tomorrow. God will help you deal with whatever hard things come up when the time comes."[1]

Remember: the most important thing is to keep the main thing the main thing! Seek *first* His kingdom.

This single adult missed a niche in history because he forgot his priorities. After graduating from college in 1756, he moved to Salisbury in the North Carolina colony and was a merchant, a justice of the peace, the king's deputy attorney, and a judge. He early became a supporter of the Patriot cause. He fought with George Washington, but was court-martialed for cowardice after the Battle of Germantown. Although he was acquitted, he resigned his command and returned to North Carolina.

In 1786, he was elected to the Continental Congress and to the Federal Convention of 1787; but for unknown reasons, he left Philadelphia before the Constitution was signed and missed a great opportunity to leave his name in history.

_____ later served three times as governor of the state of North Carolina. Despite his skills, he often drifted with the current of public opinion. His biographer noted, "In public life he sought to placate both sides." He was elected to the U.S. Senate in 1792, but he had missed his opportunity of a lifetime to sign the Constitution. Who was this single adult?[2]

> *"Obedience is the key that unlocks the treasure house of God."*
> —Belle Bennett[3]

51 Set Goals

So what are you going to do? Sit there like the proverbial bump on the log? None of us can put life on hold. Life is what happens while we wait for the right one to come along. Without goals most single adults waste this season called singleness.

Look over your life. Then ask yourself these five questions developed by Sean D. Sammon:

1: What am I doing with my life?

2: Is it possible for me to live in a way that best combines my talents, current desires, values and aspirations?

3: What do I truly get from and give to others?

4: Does anyone really care about me? Do I really care about anyone else?

5: If I were to die today, what in my life would be left unlived?[1]

Set aside some time to develop a goal—an end toward which effort and energy is directed—in each of these five areas. For example, change the wording of question 2 to an affirmation: I *can* live my life in a way that best combines my talents, current desires, values, and aspirations by. . . .

Commit yourself to realistic goals that will make the affirmation a reality.

This single adult had a simple goal expressed in a slogan, "It's about time we put someone in the governor's mansion that knows how to clean it." She began her political career stuffing envelopes as a volunteer. In 1976 she ousted an incumbent to join the Travis County, Texas, Commissioners Court. In 1982 she won a major political coup when she was elected state treasurer. She won high marks for bringing that office into the computer era; she was reelected without opposition four years later. Her goal in 1990 seemed impossible: to be elected governor of Texas. But on January 15, 1991, _____ was sworn in as the forty-fifth governor of Texas. On her sixtieth birthday she achieved another goal: a motorcycle license. She explained, tongue-in-cheek, "It's a silly thing to set a goal like getting your motorcycle license, but it really is something I've always wanted to do. It seemed totally appropriate in the sort of old-dog-new-tricks mode. It says to anyone that if you want to do it, you can do it, even when you're sixty years old!" Who is this single adult?[2]

> "I am always thrown back on the resources of God. When you are at the end of your own strength you lean so much more on God. The Holy Spirit seems to get hold of you in those times in such a way that afterwards you say, 'Wasn't that amazing? My resources are limited, but God's resources are unlimited.'"
>
> —*Eva Burrows*[3]

Some Final Words

So there you have it. Fifty-one things to do while waiting for your mate. I like the little chorus, "Love Him in the Morning," because of the words, "In the meantime and in the in-between times." That's what a lot of us are going to get: meantime and in-between times. The person we are waiting for is tied up in a committee meeting or in a traffic snarl on the interstate of life.

Maybe my sequel should be *51 Things To Be While You're Waiting for the Right One to Come Along.*

But somewhere between the "being" of single and the "doing" of single, we find our own particular mix, not unlike trying to duplicate your grandmother's favorite recipes.

Recently, I lost my friend, Anne C. Hargrove, Ph.D. in English Literature from Harvard, single parent, a deacon in my church, a woman who loved her son, her God, her church, and her world. I visited her just before she died and found her starting Tom Clancy's newest novel, *Without Remorse*. At 639 pages, it was a challenge for her to even hold the book.

"Anne," I said, "if I were dying I believe I'd be reading short stories rather than starting a long novel." She smiled, for death had taught her lessons that I have yet to learn.

When originally diagnosed with cancer, she checked out of the hospital after three days, stunning doctors by saying, "Hospitals are for sick people. "I'm going to get well." She did just that. For nine years Anne was free of cancer. During that time she wrote, *Getting Better: Conversations with Myself and Others, While Healing from Cancer*. Anne Hargrove encouraged thousands to confront their diagnosis creatively. Anne never knew the word "victim."

She had learned what the great humanitarian physician and single adult, Thomas Dooley III, had declared, "Having a fatal cancer is not important; it is *how I react* to it."[1]

While I am not comparing cancer and singleness, if I take Dooley's statement and insert the word *single*, I conclude:

Being single is not important; it is how I react to it.

I hope something in this book has captured your imagination." I hope you will apply the principles to your singleness and so live your single season that others will be encouraged and impressed. Jesus said, "I have come that (single adults) might have life," referring to eternal life. He added, "and that they might have it more abundantly." (John 10:10, KJV) Actually, I think someone left out the exclamation mark because I am certain that Jesus did not mumble the word *abundantly*. The NIV says "life . . . *to the full.*" "To the full" means living gracefully with one's singleness. That means to understand, accept and respect one's singleness.

Are you living this single season abundantly and to the fullest? Regardless of why you are single or how long you have been or will be, God's desire for every single of His unmarried children is for abundant living. First-class living.

I was moved by the story of Lei Yuille during the 1992 Los Angeles riot. Her day was interrupted by the live broadcasting of the brutal beating of trucker Reginald Denny at the fateful corner of Florence and Normandie. While others watched or shook their heads in despair at man's inhumanity to man, Yuille did something; she and her brother drove to the scene and helped save his life.[2]

You too have to do something about your season of singleness; you can't just sit around, rolling in sackcloth and ashes because the perfect mate is tardy.

My hope is that something *51 Things to Do* will help you find the courage to be the preciously unique person God says you are and that you will fully experience the outrageously extravagant grace of Jesus Christ.

Answers

1. Emily Bissell
2. Thomas Lipton
3. Adam Smith
4. Julien de Lalande Poydras
5. Dixy Ray
6. James Buchanan
7. James Montgomery, Francis R. Havergal, Isaac Watts, George Matheson, Katherine Hankey, Isaac Watts, William Cowper, Annie S. Hawks, Adelaide A. Pollard, Trans. by Catherine Winkworth
8. Clara Barton
9. Mary Wright Plummer
10. Harry T. Burn
11. Anna Jarvis
12. Sarah Josepha Hale
13. Lizzie Wooster
14. Martha Berry
15. Catherine Bruce
16. Virgina Apgar
17. Francis Marion
18. Evangeline Booth
19. Helen Keller
20. Mary Pennington
21. William Schol
22. Francis Asbury
23. Ludwig von Beethoven
24. William Travis
25. S. H. Kress
26. John Chisum
27. Katherine Lee Bates
28. Francis Ridley Havergal
29. Paul Tulane and Johns Hopkins
30. Belle Bennett
31. Mary Ann Shadd Cady
32. Rachel Carson
33. Max Cleland
34. Grover Cleveland
35. Ruth Pettigrew
36. Edith Cavell
37. Luther Rice
38. Wilbur Wright and Orville Wright
39. David Suitor
40. Alfred Nobel
41. Maxcy Gregg
42. Anna Wessel Williams
43. Dorothea Dix
44. Frank Murphy
45. Henry Martyn
46. Harry Elkins Widener
47. John Ordronaux
48. Georgia Harkness
49. Sarah Winchester
50. Alexander Martin
51. Ann Richards

Notes

Introduction

1. Kevin McCarthy, *The On-Purpose Person* (Colorado Springs: NavPress, 1993).

2. Ibid.

3. Ibid.

Chapter 1

1. *Kansas City Star,* 18 August 1993, H-5.

2. Mark Senter, *Single Adult Ministry Journal,* 95:13.

3. Francis Borden, "Merry Christmas Seals," *American Way,* 10 December 1985, 46-48.

4. Elaine Partnow, ed., *The New Quotable Woman* (New York: Facts on File, Inc., 1992), 1185.

Chapter 2

1. Alec Waugh, *The Lipton Story: A Centennial Biography* (London: Cassell, 1951), 47, 89.

2. "Corrie ten Boom: 1892-1983," booklet, memorial service for Corrie ten Boom (Old Tappan: Fleming H. Revell, 1983), 10.

Chapter 3

1. *McGraw-Hill Encyclopedia of Biography,* 1973, s.v. "Adam Smith," by John Howie.

2. L. David Duff, *The Ramsey Covenant* (Kansas City: Beacon Hill, 1982), 27.

Chapter 4

1. *Dictionary of American Biography,* 8th ed., s.v. "Julien De Lalande Poydras," (hereafter cited as DAB).

2. Rosalie Maggio, *The Beacon Book of Quotations by Women* (Boston: Beacon, 1992), 295 (hereafter cited as BBQ).

Chapter 5

1. Judith Freeman Clark, Almanac of American Women in the 20th Century (New York: Prentice-Hall, 1987), 160; *Current Biography Yearbook,* 1973, s.v. "Ray, Dixy Lee," (hereafter cited as CB).

2. John Bartlett, *Familiar Quotations,* 15th ed., ed. Emily Morison Beck (Boston: Little, Brown, 1980), 558.

Chapter 6

1. William A. DeGregorio, *The Complete Book of U.S. Presidents* (New York: Dembner Books, 1984), 213.

2. "Judith Resnik: 1949-1986," *Time,* 10 February 1986, 33.

Chapter 7

1. Lewis Grizzard, "Please, Give Him That Old Time Religion," *Tulsa World,* 13 March 1993, A-12.

2. Hugh Martin, *They Wrote Our Hymns* (London: SCM, 1961), 94.

Chapter 8

1. *The Continuum Dictionary of Women's Biography,* 1989, ed. Jennifer S. Uglow, s.v. "Barton, Clara," (hereafter cited as CDWB).

2. *BBQ,* 84.

Chapter 9

1. *DAB,* s.v. "Plummer, Mary Wright."

2. Elva McAllaster, *Free to Be Single* (Chappuqua, N.Y.: Christian Herald, 1979), 98.

Chapter 10

1. James McGinnis, "Living the Vulnerability of God," *Weavings* (July/August 1993): 43.

2. Jim Stokely and Jeff D. Johnson, eds., *An Encyclopedia of East Tennessee* (Oak Ridge, Tenn.: Children's Museum of Oak Ridge, 1981); Stanley J. Folmsbee, Robert E. Corlew, Enouch L. Mitchell, *Tennessee, A Short History* (Knoxville: University of Tennessee, 1969), 451-55.

3. Dietrich Bonhoeffer, *Life Together,* trans. John W. Doberstein (New York: Harper and Row, 1954), 97.

Chapter 11

1. Bruce Felton and Mark Fowler, *Famous Americans You Never Knew Existed* (New York: Stein and Day, 1979), 112-13.

2. Wendy Green, *Eva Burrows: Getting Things Done* (Hanks, England: Marshall Pickering, 1988), 110.

Chapter 12

1. *CDWB,* s.v. "Hale, Sarah Josepha."

2. Susan Muto, *Celebrating the Single Life* (Garden City: Doubleday, 1982), 49.

Chapter 13

1. Lisa Scott, "My Word: Perusing Obituaries Helps Put Life in Perspective," *Orlando Sentinel,* 17 June 1993, A-15.

2. James J. Fisher, "Lizzie and Her Laws Elicited Laughter, Not Respect," *Kansas City Star,* 2 September 1992, H-1.

3. J. D. Douglas, "Robert Murray McCheyene: An Influence Beyond His Years," *Decision* (March 1993): 30.

Chapter 14

1. Laubach Literacy Council brochure.

2. *DAB,* supplement 3, s.v. "Berry, Martha," 62-64; Joyce Blackburn, *Martha Berry: Little Woman with a Big Dream* (Philadelphia: Lippincott, 1968).

3. *BBQ,* 258.

Chapter 15

1. *Notable American Women: The Modern Period: A Biographical Dictionary,* vol. 1, s.v. "Bruce, Catherine Wolfe," (hereafter cited as NAW:MP vols. 1, 2, or 3).

2. CB, 1973, s.v. "Ray, Dixie"

Chapter 16

1. *NAW:MP,* s.v. "Apgar, Virginia," by Robert J. Waldinger.

2. Jesus, Luke 18:15-17, in *The Message: The New Testament in Contemporary English,* by Eugene H. Peterson (Colorado Springs: NavPress, 1993), 164-65.

Chapter 17

1. Dennis R. Miller, "Francis Marion: The Swamp Fox," *American History Illustrated* (January 1985): 34-38.

2. David A. Dryxell, "Outfiguring the Navy," *American Way* (May 1984), 43.

Chapter 18

1. Mary Troutt, *The General Was a Lady: The Story of Evangeline Booth* (Nashville: A. J. Holman, 1980), 133.

2. Eartha Mary Magdelene White Papers, Archives, University of North Florida, Jacksonville, Florida.

Chapter 19

1. *NAW:MP,* s.v. "Keller, Helen," by Joseph P. Lash.

2. Dag Hammarskjold, *Markings,* trans. Leif Sjoberg and W. H. Auden (New York: Knopf, 1965), 131.

Chapter 20

1. *NAW:MP,* s.v. "Pennington, Mary Engle," by Vivian Wiser.

2. Ida M. Tarbell, *The Business of Being a Woman* (New York: Macmillan, 1912), 176.

Chapter 21

1. Joseph J. Fucini and Suzy Fucini, *Entrepeneurs* (Boston: G. K. Hall, 1985), 22-24; Archives, Illinois College of Podiatric Medicine, Chicago, Illinois.

2. L. David Duff, *The Ramsey Covenant* (Kansas City: Beacon Hill, 1982), 28.

Chapter 22

1. L. C. Rudolph, *Francis Asbury* (Nashville: Abingdon, 1966), 107.

2. Lewis Carroll, *Through the Looking Glass* (New York: Avenel, nd.), 100.

Chapter 23

1. *New Grove Dictionary of Music and Musicians,* ed. Stanley Sadie, s.v. "Beethoven, Ludwig von," by Joseph Kerman and Alan Tyson.

2. *BBQ,* 100.

Chapter 24

1. Bill Groneman, *Alamo Defenders, A Genealogy: The People and Their Words* (Austin: Eakin, 1990), 157.

2. Francis Ridley Havergal, *Royal Bounty* (Grand Rapids: Baker, 1977), 61.

Chapter 25

1. *DAB,* supplement 5, s.v. "Kress, Stanley Henry."

2. Hugh Evan Hopkins, *Charles Simeon of Cambridge* (Grand Rapids: Eerdmans, 1977), 159.

Chapter 26

1. Jack Schaefer, *Some Good Men of the West* (New York: Houghlin-Mifflin, 1965), 164-65.

2. Eleanor L. Doan, ed., *431 Quotes from the Notes of Henrietta C. Mears* (Glendale, Calif.: Gospel Light, 1961), 85.

Chapter 27

1. Phillip Synder, *December 25: A Social History* (New York: Dodd, Mead, 1985), 122.

2. Ibid., 201.

3. Ibid., 235.

4. Charles Dickens, *A Christmas Carol* (New York: Random House, 1990), 6, 53-54.

Chapter 28

1. James M. Gordon, *Evangelical Spirituality* (London: SPCK, 1991), 196.

2. Mary Catherine DeBardelben, *Lambuth-Bennett Book of Remembrance* (Nashville: Publishing House of the Methodist Episcopal Church, South, 1922), 305.

Chapter 29

1. *DAB* V:I, s.v. "Hopkins, Johns" and "Tulane, Paul."

2. Henry David Thoreau, *Familiar Quotations,* 560.

Chapter 30

1. Carolyn L. Stapleton, "Belle Harris Bennett: Model of Holistic Christianity," *Methodist History,* 21 April 1983, 139.

2. Quoted in Richard J. Foster and James Bryan Smith, eds., *Devotional Classics* (San Francisco: Harper San Francisco, 1993), 1.

Chapter 31

1. "The Best and the Brightest," *USA Today,* 31 January 1992, 5D.

2. Carolyn Calloway-Thomas, "Cary, Mary Ann Shadd," *Black Women in America,* vol. 1, ed. Darlene Clark Hine (New York: Carlson, 1993), 224-26.

3. Norma R. Fryatt, *Sarah Josepha Hale: The Life and Times of a Nineteenth-Century Career Woman* (New York: Hawthorne, 1975), 25.

Chapter 32

1. Wendell Berry, *What Are People For?* (San Francisco: North Point, 1990), 97.

2. Ibid., 98.

3. *NAW:MP,* s.v. "Carson, Rachel Louise," by Paul Brooks.

4. Marci DeWolf, "Global Frontrunners: First Lady of the Everglades," *Profiles* (April 1993): 14.

Chapter 33

1. "Cleland, Max," *Contemporary Authors,* vol. 11, ed. Hal May (Detroit: Gale, 1985), 94; Carl T. Rowan, "Words That Gave Us Strength," *Reader's Digest* (April 1987): 55-56.

2. Blackburn, *Martha Berry,* 152.

Chapter 34

1. *American Heritage Pictorial History of the Presidents of the United States,* s.v. "Cleveland, Grover" (New York: American Heritage Publishing, 1968), 553-62; *DAB* 2:1, s.v. "Cleveland, Grover."

2. Elva McAllaster, *Free to Be Single* (Chappuqua, N.Y.: Christian Herald, 1979), 79.

Chapter 35

1. Catherine Allen, "Ruth Pettigrew: Pioneer to the People," unpublished paper, Southern Baptist Historical Commission.

2. Dag Hammarsjkold, *Markings,* trans. Leif Sjoberg and W. H. Auden (New York: Knopf, 1965), 131.

Chapter 36

1. *International Dictionary of 20th-Century Biography,* 1987, eds. Edward Vernon and Rima Shore, s.v. "Cavell, Edith Louisa," (hereafter cited as ID2B).

2. R. E. B. Baylor Papers, Archives, Baylor University.

Chapter 37

1. Evelyn Wingo Thompson, *Luther Rice: Believer in Tomorrow* (Nashville: Broadman, 1967).

2. Anna Louise Strong in BBQ, 25.

Chapter 38

1. ID2B, s.v. "Wright, Wilbur and Orville."

2. Eugenia Price, *Just As I Am* (Philadelphia: Lippincott, 1968), 145.

Chapter 39

1. Robert Fulghum, *Maybe, Maybe Not* (New York: Villard, 1993), 226.

2. Ibid.

3. Muto, *Celebrating,* 144–45.

Chapter 40

1. Michael Evlanoff and Marjorie Fluor, *Alfred Nobel: The Loneliest Millionaire* (New York: Ward Richie Press, 1969), 4–5, 218.

2. A. A. Bonar, *Robert Murray McCheyne* (Grand Rapids: Zondervan, 1983), 41.

Chapter 41

1. *DAB,* IV: 1, s.v. "Gregg, Maxcy."

2. Mary Schmich, "At Long Last," *Arizona Republic,* 20 April 1986, A-2.

Chapter 42

1. *NAW:MP*, s.v. "Williams, Anna Wessels," by Elizabeth D. Robinson.

2. *NAW:MP*, s.v. "Apgar, Virginia," by Robert J. Waldinger.

Chapter 43

1. *NAW 1*, s.v. "Dix, Dorothea Lynde," by Helen E. Marshall.

2. *Letters from Lillian* (Springfield, Mo.: Assemblies of God, 1983), 104.

Chapter 44

1. *DAB*, supplement 4, s.v. "Murphy, Frank."
2. Susan Warner in *NQW*, 189.

Chapter 45

1. Brian L. Harbour, *Famous Singles of the Bible* (Nashville: Broadman, 1980), preface.

2. Constance Padwick, *Henry Martyn* (Chicago: Moody, 1980).

3. Barbara Hudson Powers, *The Henrietta Mears Story* (Old Tappan, N.J.: Revell, 1965), 58.

Chapter 46

1. *DAB*, X:2, s.v. "Widener, Harry Elkins."
2. Wendy Wasserstein in *BBQ*, 12.

Chapter 47

1. *DAB*, VII:2, s.v. "Ordronaux, John."
2. Helen Keller in *BBQ*, 297.

Chapter 48

1. *NAW:MP*, s.v. "Harkness, Georgia Elma," by Dorothy C. Bass.

2. *CB*, 1974, Barbara Jordan.

Chapter 49

1. Nancy Woods, *Spirit Walker* (New York: Doubleday, 1993), 59.

2. Michele Burgess, "West Coast Spirits," *Alaska Airlines* magazine, (May 1989): 40-41;

Ralph Rambo, *Lady of Mystery: Sarah Winchester* (Rambo, 1967).

3. Evangeline Booth in *Topical Encyclopedia of Living Quotations,* ed. Sherwood Wirt (Minneapolis: Bethany, 1982), 5.

Chapter 50

1. Sean D. Sammon, *An Undivided Heart: Making Sense of Celibacy and Chastity* (New York: Alba House, 1993), 12.

2. Stefanie Scott, "Richards Gets Ticket to Ride," *The San Antonio Express-News,* 2 September 1993, 13A.

3. Green, *Eva Burrows,* 175.

Chapter 51

1. Peterson, *The Message,* 21.

2. *DAB,* VI:2, s.v. "Martin, Alexander."

3. DeBardelben, *Lambuth-Bennett Book of Remembrance,* 145.

Some Final Words

1. Lucille Selsor, *"Sincerely Tom Dooley"* (New York: Twin Circle, 1969), 86.

2. "Four Tell of Rush to Save Beaten Trucker," *Kansas City Star,* 27 August 1993, A-5.